The British System
of Government

London: H M S O

Researched and written by Reference Services, Central Office of Information.

ISBN 0 11 701839 2

HMSO publications are available from:

HMSO Publications Centre
(Mail, fax and telephone orders only)
PO Box 276, London SW8 5DT
Telephone orders 071-873 9090
General enquiries 071-873 0011
(queuing system in operation for both numbers)
Fax orders 071-873 8200

HMSO Bookshops
49 High Holborn, London WC1V 6HB   071-873 0011
Fax 071-873 8200 (counter service only)
258 Broad Street, Birmingham B1 2HE   021-643 3740   Fax 021-643 6510
Southey House, 33 Wine Street, Bristol BS1 2BQ
0272 264306   Fax 0272 294515
9-21 Princess Street, Manchester M60 8AS   061-834 7201   Fax 061-833 0634
16 Arthur Street, Belfast BT1 4GD   0232 238451   Fax 0232 235401
71 Lothian Road, Edinburgh EH3 9AZ   031-228 4181   Fax 031-229 2734

HMSO's Accredited Agents
(see Yellow Pages)

and through good booksellers

Cover photograph credit
COI Pictures

Contents

Introduction

This book describes the British system of government against the background of its historical development over the centuries. It focuses on the relationships between the different organs of government: the legislature (Parliament), the executive (headed by the Government), and the judiciary.

The book also gives brief descriptions of the systems of government in Scotland, Wales, Northern Ireland, the Isle of Man and the Channel Islands. In each case there is a brief account of the history of the relationship with England or, later, Britain.[1] Britain's relationship with the European Union is also described.

---

[1] The term 'Britain' is used informally in this book to mean the United Kingdom of Great Britain and Northern Ireland; 'Great Britain' comprises England, Wales and Scotland.

The Development of the British System of Government

The growth of political institutions in England can be traced back to the period of Saxon rule, which lasted from the fifth century AD, until the Norman Conquest in 1066. This period saw the origins of the institution of kingship, and of the idea that the king should seek the advice of a council of prominent men. The Saxons also established a network of local government areas, including shires (counties) and burghs (boroughs), which continue to influence the structure of local government.

The period of Norman rule after 1066 saw a considerable strengthening of royal control. However, the monarchy eventually experienced difficulties in controlling the growing machinery of government. The actions of King John (1199–1216) led to opposition from feudal barons and leading figures in the Church. In 1215 the barons forced the King to agree to a series of concessions embodied in a charter which became known as Magna Carta. The charter, which provided for the protection of the rights of feudal proprietors against the abuse of royal power, came to be regarded as the key expression of the rights of the community against the Crown.

The term 'Parliament' was first officially used in 1236 to describe the gathering of feudal barons and representatives of counties and towns which the king summoned if extraordinary taxation was required. By the 15th century Parliament had acquired the right to make laws (see p. 14).

A clash between the monarchy, which insisted on its divine right to rule, and Parliament, which insisted on its legislative authority, led to the outbreak of the Civil War in 1642. Following the defeat of the royalist armies and the execution of Charles I in 1649, the monarchy and the House of Lords were abolished and the country was proclaimed a republic. However, the republican experiment came to an end in 1660, two years after the death of the 'Lord Protector', Oliver Cromwell. Charles I's son was restored to the throne as Charles II.

Charles II's successor, James II (1685–88), attempted to rule without the consent of Parliament. As a result, in 1688 a group of leading men invited William of Orange (a grandson of Charles I and husband of Mary, James II's eldest daughter) to 'secure the infringed liberties' of the country. James II fled into exile. Following the success of the revolution of 1688, Parliament in 1689 passed the Bill of Rights, which made it impracticable for the Sovereign to ignore the wishes of Parliament. However, the monarch continued to be at the centre of executive power. To enable the Sovereign and Parliament to work together to carry on the government of the country, a group of ministers, or Cabinet, became the link between the executive and the legislature. Although the ministers were appointed by the Sovereign, they had to have sufficient support in the House of Commons to enable them to persuade Parliament to pass legislation and vote for taxation.

A few years after the accession to the throne of George I in 1714, the monarch ceased to attend Cabinet meetings and none of his successors did thereafter. Instead, the Cabinet was presided over by the First Lord of the Treasury, who came to be known as the Prime Minister. After that the individual influence of the monarch in exercising executive power declined with a corresponding increase in that of the Cabinet as a whole. Sir Robert Peel, Prime Minister from 1841 to 1846, was probably the first holder of this office to perform a role similar to that of a modern Prime Minister. Since the mid-19th century the Prime Minister has normally been the leader of the party with a majority in the House of Commons.

The Reform Act 1832 reformed the system of parliamentary representation, which dated from medieval times. It also standardised the qualifications for the right to vote. The Act started a train of events which led to all adults (with a few exceptions—see p. 19) receiving the vote and direct popular control over the House of Commons, a process which was completed early in the 20th century.

The British Constitution

The British constitution is, to a large extent, a product of the historical events described above, and has thus evolved over many centuries. Unlike the constitutions of most other countries, it is not set out in any single document. Instead it is made up of statute law, common law (see p. 77) and conventions. (Conventions are rules and practices which are not legally enforceable but which are regarded as indispensable to the working of government; many are derived from the historical events described above.)

The constitution can be altered by Act of Parliament, or by general agreement to alter a convention. It is thus adaptable to changing political conditions.

The organs of government overlap but can be clearly distinguished. Parliament is the legislature and the supreme authority. The executive consists of:

—the Government: the Cabinet and other ministers responsible for national policies;

—government departments, responsible for national administration;

—local authorities, responsible for many local services; and public corporations, responsible for operating particular nationalised industries or other bodies, subject to ministerial control.

The judiciary determines common law and interprets statutes.

The Monarchy

The monarchy is the oldest institution of government, going back to at least the ninth century-four centuries before Parliament and three centuries before the law courts.[2] Queen Elizabeth II is herself directly descended from King Egbert, who united England under his rule in 829. The only interruption in the history of the monarchy was the republic, which lasted from 1649 to 1660 (see p. 3).

Today the Queen is not only Britain's head of State, but also an important symbol of national unity. The royal title in Britain is: 'Elizabeth the Second, by the Grace of God of the United Kingdom of Great Britain and Northern Ireland and of Her other Realms and Territories Queen, Head of the Commonwealth, Defender of the Faith'. In the Channel Islands (see p. 101) and the Isle of Man (see p. 104) the Queen is represented by a Lieutenant-Governor.

The Commonwealth

Although the seat of the monarchy is in Britain, the Queen is also head of State of a number of Commonwealth states. These include Australia, Barbados, Canada, Jamaica, New Zealand and Papua New Guinea. In each such state the Queen is represented by a Governor-General, appointed by her on the advice of the ministers of the country concerned and completely independent of the British Government. Other member states are republics or have their own monarchies.

---

[2] For further details see *The Monarchy* (Aspects of Britain: HMSO, 1991).

In British dependent territories the Queen is usually represented by a governor who is responsible to the British Government for the administration of the country concerned.

Succession

The title to the Crown is derived partly from statute and partly from common law rules of descent. Despite interruptions in the direct line of succession, the hereditary principle upon which it was founded has always been preserved.

Sons of the Sovereign have precedence over daughters in succeeding to the throne. When a daughter succeeds, she becomes Queen Regnant, and has the same powers as a king. The consort of a king takes her husband's rank and style, becoming Queen. The constitution does not give any special rank or privileges to the husband of a Queen Regnant, although in practice he fills an important role in the life of the nation, as does the Duke of Edinburgh.

Under the Act of Settlement of 1700, which formed part of the Revolution Settlement following the events of 1688 (see p. 3), only Protestant descendants of a granddaughter of James I of England and VI of Scotland (Princess Sophia, the Electress of Hanover) are eligible to succeed. The order of succession can be altered only by common consent of the countries of the Commonwealth.

Accession

The Sovereign succeeds to the throne as soon as his or her predecessor dies: there is no interregnum. The successor is at once proclaimed at an Accession Council, to which all members of the Privy Council (see p. 98) are summoned. The Lords Spiritual and Temporal (see p. 16), the Lord Mayor and Aldermen, and other leading citizens of the City of London, are also invited. The origins of this act of recognition can be traced back to the Anglo-Saxon practice whereby the Witan or Council elected the king from among the members of the royal family.

Coronation

The Sovereign's coronation follows the accession after a convenient interval. The ceremony takes place at Westminster Abbey in London, in the presence of representatives of the Houses of Parliament and of all the great public organisations in Britain. The Prime Ministers and leading members of the other Commonwealth nations and representatives of other countries also attend.

The Monarch's Role in Government

The Queen personifies the State. In law, she is head of the executive, an integral part of the legislature, head of the judiciary, the commander-in-chief of all the armed forces of the Crown and the 'supreme governor' of the established Church of England. As a result of a long process of evolution during which the monarchy's absolute power has been progressively reduced (see pp. 2–4), the Queen acts on the advice of her ministers. Britain is governed by Her Majesty's Government in the name of the Queen.

Within this framework, and in spite of a trend during the past hundred years towards giving powers directly to ministers, the Queen still takes part in some important acts of government. These include summoning, proroguing (discontinuing until the next session without dissolution) and dissolving Parliament; and giving Royal Assent to Bills passed by Parliament. The Queen also formally appoints many important office holders, including government ministers, judges, officers in the armed forces, diplomats, bishops and some other senior clergy of the Church of England. She is also involved in pardoning people convicted of crimes; and conferring peerages, knighthoods and other honours.

One of the Queen's most important functions is appointing the Prime Minister: by convention the Queen invites the leader of the political party which commands a majority in the House of Commons to form a government. In international affairs the Queen, as head of State, has the power to declare war and make peace, to recognise foreign states and governments, to conclude treaties and to annex or cede territory.

With rare exceptions (such as appointing the Prime Minister), acts involving the use of 'royal prerogative' powers are nowadays performed by government ministers, who are responsible to Parliament and can be questioned about particular policies. Parliamentary authority is not required for the exercise of these prerogative powers, although Parliament may restrict or abolish such rights.

The Queen continues to play an important role in the working of government. She holds Privy Council meetings, gives audiences to her ministers and officials in Britain and overseas, receives accounts of Cabinet decisions, reads dispatches and signs state papers. She must be consulted on every aspect of national life, and must show complete impartiality.

Provision has been made to appoint a regent to perform these royal functions should the Queen be totally incapacitated. The regent would be the Queen's eldest son, the Prince of Wales, then those, in order of succession to the throne, who are of age. In the event of her partial incapacity or absence abroad, the Queen may delegate certain royal functions to the Counsellors of State (the Duke of Edinburgh, the four adults next in line of succession, and the Queen Mother). However, Counsellors of State may not, for instance, dissolve Parliament (except on the Queen's instructions), nor create peers.

Ceremonial and Royal Visits

Ceremonial has always been associated with the British monarchy, and, in spite of changes in the outlook of both the Sovereign and the people, many traditional ceremonies continue to take place. Royal marriages and royal funerals are marked by public ceremony and the Sovereign's birthday is officially celebrated in June by Trooping the Colour on Horse Guards Parade. State banquets take place when a foreign monarch or head of State visits Britain; investitures are held at Buckingham Palace and the Palace of Holyroodhouse in Edinburgh to bestow honours; and royal processions add significance to such occasions as a state opening of Parliament.

Each year the Queen and other members of the royal family visit many parts of Britain. Their presence at events of national and local importance attracts considerable interest. The Queen pays state visits to foreign governments, accompanied by the Duke of Edinburgh. She also tours the other countries of the Commonwealth. Other members of the royal family pay official visits overseas, occasionally representing the Queen, or often in connection with an organisation with which they are associated.

Royal Income and Expenditure

Until 1760 the Sovereign had to provide for the payment of all government expenses, including the salaries of officials, and the expenses of the royal palaces and households. These were met from hereditary revenues, mainly income from Crown lands, and income

from some customs duties, certain taxes and postal revenues granted to the monarch by Parliament. The income from these sources
eventually proved inadequate and, when George III became King
in 1760, he turned over to the Government most of the hereditary
revenue. In return he received an annual grant (Civil List) from
which he continued to pay the royal expenditure of a personal char-
acter and also the salaries of government officials, and certain pensions. The latter charges were removed from the Civil List in 1830.

Present Arrangements

Today the expenditure incurred by the Queen in carrying out her
public duties is financed from the Civil List and from government
departments (which meet the cost of, for example, the Royal Yacht
and the aircraft of the Queen's Flight). All such expenditure is
approved by Parliament. In January 1991 Civil List payments were
fixed at £7.9 million a year for ten years. About three-quarters of
the Queen's Civil List provision is required to meet the cost of
staff. These deal with, among other things, state papers and corre-
spondence, and the organisation of state occasions, visits and other
public engagements undertaken by the Queen in Britain and overseas. The Queen's private expenditure as Sovereign is met from the
Privy Purse, which is financed mainly from the revenue of the
Duchy of Lancaster; her expenditure as a private individual is met
from her own personal resources.

Taxation

Since April 1993 the Queen has voluntarily paid income tax on all
her personal income and on that part of the Privy Purse income
which is used for private purposes. The Queen also pays tax on any
realised capital gains on her private investments and on the private

proportion of assets in the Privy Purse. Inheritance tax will not, however, apply to transfers from one sovereign to his or her successor, although any personal bequests other than to the successor will be subject to inheritance tax. In line with these changes the Prince of Wales pays income tax on the income from the Duchy of Cornwall to the extent that it is used for private purposes.

Under the Civil List Acts, other members of the royal family also receive annual parliamentary allowances to enable them to carry out their public duties. The Prince of Wales, however, receives no such allowance, since as Duke of Cornwall he is entitled to the income of the estate of the Duchy of Cornwall. Each year the Queen pays the Government a sum equivalent to that provided by Parliament for all members of the royal family, except the Queen Mother and the Duke of Edinburgh.

Parliament: the Legislature

Origins of Parliament

The medieval kings were expected to meet all royal expenses, private and public, out of their own revenue. If extra resources were needed for an emergency, such as a war, the Sovereign would seek to persuade his barons, in the Great Council—a gathering of leading men which met several times a year—to grant an aid. During the 13th century several kings found the private revenues and baronial aids insufficient to meet the expenses of government. They therefore summoned to the Great Council not only the great feudal magnates but also representatives of counties, cities and towns, primarily to get their assent to extraordinary taxation. In this way the Great Council came to include those who were summoned by name (those who, broadly speaking, were to form the House of Lords) and those who were representatives of communities (the commons). The two parts, together with the Sovereign, eventually became known as 'Parliament'. (The first official use of this term, which originally meant a meeting for parley or discussion, was in 1236.)[3]

Over the course of time, the commons began to realise the strength of their position. By the middle of the 14th century the formula had appeared which in substance was the same as that used nowadays in voting supplies to the Crown—that is, money to the Government—namely, 'by the Commons with the advice of the

[3] For further details, see *Parliament* (Aspects of Britain: HMSO, 1994).

Lords Spiritual and Temporal'. In 1407 Henry IV pledged that henceforth all money grants should be approved by the House of Commons before being considered by the House of Lords.

A similar advance was made in the legislative field. Originally the King's legislation needed only the assent of his councillors. Starting with the right of individual commoners to present petitions, the Commons as a body gained the right to submit collective petitions. Later, during the 15th century, they gained the right to participate in giving their requests—their 'Bills'—the form of law.

The subsequent development of the power of the House of Commons was built upon these foundations. The constitutional developments of the 17th century (see p. 3) led to Parliament securing its position as the supreme legislative authority.

The Powers of Parliament

The three elements which make up Parliament—the Queen, the House of Lords and the elected House of Commons—are constituted on different principles. They meet together only on occasions of symbolic significance such as the state opening of Parliament, when the Commons are summoned by the Queen to the House of Lords. The agreement of all three elements is normally required for legislation, but that of the Queen is given as a matter of course to Bills sent to her.

Parliament can legislate for Britain as a whole, or for any part of the country. It can also legislate for the Channel Islands (see p. 101) and the Isle of Man (see p. 104), which are Crown dependencies and not part of Britain. They have local legislatures which make laws on island affairs.

As there are no legal restraints imposed by a written constitution, Parliament may legislate as it pleases, subject to Britain's obligations as a member of the European Union. It can make or change any law; and can overturn established conventions or turn them into law. It can even prolong its own life beyond the normal period without consulting the electorate.

In practice, however, Parliament does not assert its supremacy in this way. Its members bear in mind the common law (see p. 77) and normally act in accordance with precedent. The House of Commons is directly responsible to the electorate, and in this century the House of Lords has recognised the supremacy of the elected chamber. The system of party government helps to ensure that Parliament legislates with its responsibility to the electorate in mind.

The Functions of Parliament

The main functions of Parliament are:

—to pass laws;

—to provide, by voting for taxation, the means of carrying on the work of government;

—to scrutinise government policy and administration, including proposals for expenditure; and

—to debate the major issues of the day.

In carrying out these functions Parliament helps to bring the relevant facts and issues before the electorate. By custom, Parliament is also informed before all important international treaties and agreements are ratified. The making of treaties is, however, a royal prerogative exercised on the advice of the Government and is not subject to parliamentary approval.

The Meeting of Parliament

A Parliament has a maximum duration of five years, but in practice general elections are usually held before the end of this term. The maximum life has been prolonged by legislation in rare circumstances such as the two world wars. Parliament is dissolved and writs for a general election are ordered by the Queen on the advice of the Prime Minister.

The life of a Parliament is divided into sessions. Each usually lasts for one year—normally beginning and ending in October or November. There are 'adjournments' at night, at weekends, at Christmas, Easter and the late Spring Bank Holiday, and during a long summer break starting in late July or early August. The average number of 'sitting' days in a session is about 160 in the House of Commons and about 145 in the House of Lords. At the start of each session the Queen's speech to Parliament outlines the Government's policies and proposed legislative programme. Each session is ended by prorogation. Parliament then 'stands prorogued' for about a week until the new session opens. Public Bills which have not been passed by the end of the session are lost.

The House of Lords

The House of Lords consists of the Lords Spiritual and the Lords Temporal. The Lords Spiritual are the Archbishops of Canterbury and York and 24 senior bishops of the Church of England. The Lords Temporal consist of:

—all hereditary peers and peeresses of England, Scotland, Great Britain and the United Kingdom (but not peers of Ireland);

—life peers created to assist the House in its judicial duties (Lords of Appeal or 'law lords'); and

—all other life peers.

Hereditary peerages carry a right to sit in the House provided holders establish their claim and are aged 21 years or over. However, anyone succeeding to a peerage may, within 12 months of succession, disclaim that peerage for his or her lifetime.

Peerages, both hereditary and life, are created by the Sovereign on the advice of the Prime Minister. They are usually granted in recognition of service in politics or other walks of life or because one of the political parties wishes to have the recipient in the House of Lords. The House also provides a place in Parliament for people who offer useful advice, but do not wish to be involved in party politics. In addition, senior judges are given life peerages as Lords of Appeal. The House of Lords is the final court of appeal for civil cases in Britain and for criminal cases in England, Wales and Northern Ireland (see p. 79).

In early April 1994 there were 1,202 members of the House of Lords, including the two archbishops and 24 bishops. The Lords Temporal consisted of 759 hereditary peers who had succeeded to their titles, 15 hereditary peers who had had their titles conferred on them (including the Prince of Wales), and 402 life peers, of whom 21 who were 'law lords'.

Officers of the House of Lords
The House is presided over by the Lord Chancellor, who takes his place on the woolsack as ex-officio Speaker of the House. In his absence his place is taken by a deputy. The first of the deputy speakers is the Chairman of Committees, who is appointed at the beginning of each session, and normally chairs most committees.

The Clerk of the Parliaments is responsible for the records of proceedings of the House of Lords and for the text of Acts of Parliament. He is the accounting officer for the cost of the House, and is in charge of the administrative staff of the House, known as the Parliament Office. The Gentleman Usher of the Black Rod, usually known as 'Black Rod', is responsible for security, accommodation and services in the House of Lords' part of the Palace of Westminster.

The House of Commons

The House of Commons is elected by universal adult suffrage and consists of 651 Members of Parliament (MPs). In early April 1994 there were 59 women, three Asian and three black MPs. Of the 651 seats, 524 are for England, 38 for Wales, 72 for Scotland, and 17 for Northern Ireland.

General elections are held after a Parliament has been dissolved and a new one summoned by the Queen. When an MP dies or resigns, or is given a peerage, a by-election takes place. Members are paid a basic annual salary of £31,687 (from January 1994) and an office costs allowance of up to £40,380. There are also a number of other allowances.

Office of the House of Commons

The chief officer of the House of Commons is the Speaker, elected by MPs to preside over the House. Other officers include the Chairman of Ways and Means and two deputy chairmen, who act as Deputy Speakers. They are elected by the House on the nomination of the Government but are drawn from the Opposition as well as the government party. They, like the Speaker, neither speak nor vote other than in their official capacity. Overall responsibility for the administration of the House rests with the House of Commons Commission, a statutory body chaired by the Speaker.

Permanent officers (who are not MPs) include the Clerk of the House of Commons, who is the principal adviser to the Speaker on its privileges and procedures. The Clerk is also accounting officer for the House. The Serjeant-at-Arms, who waits on the Speaker, carries out certain orders of the House; he is also the official housekeeper of the Commons' part of the building, and is responsible for security. Other officers serve the House in the Library, the Department of the Official Report (Hansard), the Finance and Administration Department and the Refreshment Department.

Parliamentary Electoral System

For electoral purposes Britain is divided into constituencies, each of which returns one member to the House of Commons.[4] To ensure that constituency electorates are kept roughly equal, four permanent Parliamentary Boundary Commissions, one each for England, Wales, Scotland and Northern Ireland, keep constituencies under review. They recommend any adjustment of seats that may seem necessary in the light of population movements or other changes. Elections are by secret ballot.

Who May Vote
British citizens, together with citizens of other Commonwealth countries and citizens of the Irish Republic resident in Britain, may vote provided they are:

—aged 18 or over,

—included in the annual register of electors for the constituency and

—not subject to any disqualification.

[4] For further details, see *Parliamentary Elections* (Aspects of Britain: HMSO, 1991).

Members of the armed forces, Crown servants and staff of the British Council employed overseas (together with their wives or husbands if accompanying them) may be registered for an address in the constituency where they would live but for their service. The Representation of the People Act 1989 extended the right to vote for British citizens living abroad by increasing from 5 to 20 years the period during which they may apply to be registered to vote.

Voting Procedures

Each elector may cast one vote, normally in person at a polling station. Electors whose circumstances on polling day are such that they cannot reasonably be expected to vote in person at their local polling station—for example, electors away on holiday—may apply for an absent vote at a particular election. Electors who are physically incapacitated or unable to vote in person because of the nature of their work, or because they have moved to a new area, may apply for an indefinite absent vote. People entitled to an absent vote may vote by post or by proxy, although postal ballot papers cannot be sent to addresses outside Britain.

Voting is not compulsory; 76.9 per cent of a total electorate of 43.3 million people voted in the general election in April 1992. The simple majority system of voting is used. Candidates are elected if they have more votes than any of the other candidates (although not necessarily an absolute majority over all other candidates).

Candidates

British citizens and citizens of other Commonwealth countries, together with citizens of the Irish Republic, may stand for election as MPs provided they are aged 21 or over and are not disqualified. A candidate's nomination for election must be proposed and seconded by two electors registered as voters in the constituency and signed by eight other electors.

Candidates do not have to be backed by a political party. A candidate must also deposit £500, which is returned if he or she receives 5 per cent or more of the votes cast.

The maximum sum a candidate may spend on a general election campaign is £4,642, plus 3.9 pence for each elector in a borough constituency or 5.2 pence for each elector in a county constituency. Higher limits have been set for by-elections in order to reflect the fact that they are often regarded as tests of national opinion in the period between general elections. A candidate may post an election address to each elector in the constituency, free of charge. All election expenses, apart from the candidate's personal expenses, are subject to the statutory limit.

The Political Party System

The party system, which has existed in one form or another since the 18th century, is an essential element in the working of the constitution.[5]

The present system depends upon the existence of organised political parties, each of which presents its policies to the electorate for approval. The parties are not registered or formally recognised in law, but in practice most candidates in elections—and almost all winning candidates—belong to one of the main parties.

For the last 150 years a predominantly two-party system has existed. Since 1945 either the Conservative Party, whose origins go back to the 18th century, or the Labour Party, which emerged in the last decade of the 19th century, has held power. A new party—

[5] For further details, see *Organisation of Political Parties* (Aspects of Britain: HMSO, 1994).

the Liberal Democrats—was formed in 1988 when the Liberal Party, which could trace its origins to the 18th century, merged with the Social Democratic Party (formed in 1981). Other parties include two nationalist parties, Plaid Cymru (founded in Wales in 1925) and the Scottish National Party (founded in 1934). In Northern Ireland there are a number of parties. They include the Ulster Unionist Party, formed in the early part of this century; the Democratic Unionist Party, founded in 1971 by a group which broke away from the Ulster Unionists; and the Social Democratic and Labour Party, founded in 1970.

Since 1945 eight general elections have been won by the Conservative Party and six by the Labour Party; the great majority of members of the House of Commons have belonged to one of these two parties. Table 1 shows the results of the last general election.

Table 1: Results of the April 1992 General Election

Party	Members elected
Conservative	336
Labour	271
Liberal Democrats	20
Plaid Cymru (Welsh Nationalist)	4
Scottish National	3
Ulster Unionist (Northern Ireland)	9
Ulster Democratic Unionist (Northern Ireland)	3
Ulster Popular Unionist (Northern Ireland)	1
Social Democratic and Labour (Northern Ireland)	4
Total	651

The party which wins most seats (although not necessarily the most votes) at a general election, or which has the support of a majority of members in the House of Commons, usually forms the Government. By tradition, the leader of the majority party is asked by the Sovereign to form a government. About 100 of its members in the House of Commons and the House of Lords receive ministerial appointments (including appointment to the Cabinet—see p. 39) on the advice of the Prime Minister. The largest minority party becomes the official Opposition, with its own leader and 'shadow cabinet'.

The Party System in Parliament

Leaders of the Government and Opposition sit on the front benches of the Commons with their supporters (the backbenchers) sitting behind them.

The effectiveness of the party system in Parliament rests largely on the relationship between the Government and the opposition parties. Depending on the relative strengths of the parties in the House of Commons, the Opposition may seek to overthrow the Government by defeating it in a vote on a 'matter of confidence'. In general, however, its aims are to contribute to the formulation of policy and legislation by constructive criticism; to oppose government proposals it considers objectionable; to seek amendments to government Bills; and to put forward its own policies in order to improve its chances of winning the next general election.

Government business arrangements are settled, under the direction of the Prime Minister and the Leaders of the two Houses, by the Government Chief Whip in consultation with the Opposition Chief Whip. The Chief Whips together constitute the 'usual channels' often referred to when the question of finding time for a particular item of business is discussed. The Leaders of the two Houses are responsible for enabling the Houses to debate matters about which they are concerned.

Outside Parliament, party control is exercised by the national and local organisations. Inside, it is exercised by the Chief Whips and their assistants, who are chosen within the party. Their duties include keeping members informed of forthcoming parliamentary business, maintaining the party's voting strength by ensuring members attend important debates, and passing on to the party leadership the opinions of backbench members. The Whips indicate the importance their party attaches to a vote on a particular issue by underlining items of business (once, twice or three times) on the notice sent to MPs. In the Commons, failure to comply with a 'three-line whip' (the most important) is usually seen as a rebellion against the party. Party discipline tends to be less strong in the Lords than in the Commons, since Lords have less hope of high office and no need of party support in elections.

Financial Assistance to Parties

Annual assistance from public funds helps opposition parties carry out their parliamentary work at Westminster. It is limited to parties which had at least two members elected at the previous general election or one member elected and a minimum of 150,000 votes cast.

From April 1994 the amount is £3,442.50 for every seat won, plus £6.89 for every 200 votes. The amounts are to be increased annually by reference to the retail prices index.

Parliamentary Procedure

Parliamentary procedure is based on custom and precedent, partly codified by each House in its Standing Orders. The system of debate is similar in both Houses. Every subject starts off as a proposal or 'motion' by a member. After debate, the Speaker or Chairman 'puts the question' whether to agree with the motion or not. The question may be decided without voting, or by a simple majority vote. The main difference of procedure between the two Houses is that the Speaker or Chairman in the Lords has no powers of order; instead such matters are decided by the general feeling of the House. In the Commons the Speaker has full authority to enforce the rules of the House.

The Speaker supervises voting in the Commons and announces the final result. In a tied vote the Speaker gives a casting vote. The voting procedure in the House of Lords is broadly similar.

The Commons has a public register of MPs' financial interests. Members with a financial interest in a debate in the House must declare it when speaking. There is no register of financial interests in the Lords, but Lords speaking in a debate in which they have a direct interest are expected to declare it. Lords, by custom, speak 'on their honour'.

Proceedings of both Houses are normally public. The minutes and speeches (transcribed verbatim in Hansard) are published daily.

The records of the Lords from 1497 and of the Commons from 1547, are available to the public through the House of Lords Record Office.

The proceedings of both Houses of Parliament may be broadcast on television and radio, either live or, more usually, in recorded or edited form. Complete coverage is available on cable television.

The Law-making Process
The law undergoes constant reform in the courts (see p. 77) as established principles are clarified or reapplied to meet new circumstances. Fundamental changes are the responsibility of

Parliament and the Government through the normal legislative process.

Draft laws take the form of parliamentary Bills. Most are public Bills involving measures relating to public policy. Public Bills can be introduced, in either House, by a government minister or by an ordinary ('private' or 'backbench') member. Most public Bills that become law are sponsored by the Government.

Before a government Bill is drafted, there may be consultation with professional bodies, voluntary organisations and other agencies interested in the subject, and interest groups and pressure groups which seek to promote specific causes. Proposals for legislative changes are sometimes set out in government 'White Papers' which may be debated in Parliament before a Bill is introduced. From time to time consultation papers, sometimes called 'Green Papers', set out government proposals which are still taking shape and seek comments from the public.

Bills must normally be passed by both Houses. Government Bills likely to raise political controversy usually go through the Commons before being discussed in the Lords, while those of a technical but non-political nature often pass through the Lords first. A Bill with a mainly financial purpose is nearly always introduced in the Commons, and a Bill involving taxation must be based on resolutions agreed by that House, often after debate, before it can be introduced. If the main object of a Bill is to create a public charge (that is, new taxation or public spending), it must be introduced by a government minister in the Commons or, if brought from the Lords, be taken up by a government minister. This gives the Government considerable control over financial legislation.

Private Members' Bills

At the beginning of each session private members of the Commons ballot (draw lots) for the opportunity to introduce a Bill on one of the Fridays specially allocated; the first 20 are successful. Private members may also present a Bill after question time (see p. 29). They may also seek to introduce a Bill under the 'ten minute rule'. This allows two speeches, one in favour of and one against the measure. Private members' Bills often do not proceed very far, but a few become law each session. Private members' Bills may be introduced in the House of Lords at any time, but when they come to the Commons they do not proceed further unless taken up by a private member.

Passage of Public Bills

The process of passing a public Bill is similar in both Houses. On introduction, the Bill receives a first reading, without debate and is printed. After between one day and several weeks, depending on the nature of the Bill, it is given a second reading after a debate on its general principles. After a second reading in the Commons, a Bill is usually referred to a standing committee for detailed examination (see p. 30). The committee stage is followed by the report stage in the whole House, during which further amendments may be considered. At the third reading a Bill is reviewed in its final form and may be debated again.

After the third reading a Commons Bill is sent to the Lords. Once it has received a second reading in the Lords, a Bill is normally considered by a committee of the whole House. It is then considered on report and read a third time. At all these stages amendments may be made.

A Bill which starts in the Lords and is passed by that House is then sent to the Commons for all its stages there. Amendments made by the second House must generally be agreed by the first, or a compromise reached, before a Bill can become law.

Royal Assent

When a Bill has passed through all its parliamentary stages, it is sent to the Queen for Royal Assent, after which it is part of the law of the land and known as an Act of Parliament. The Royal Assent has not been refused since 1707.

Limitations on the Power of the Lords

Most government Bills introduced and passed in the Lords pass through the Commons without difficulty, but a Lords Bill which was unacceptable to the Commons would not become law. The Lords, on the other hand, do not generally prevent Bills insisted upon by the Commons from becoming law, though they will often amend them and return them for further consideration by the Commons.

By convention, the Lords pass Bills authorising taxation or national expenditure without amendment. Under the Parliament Acts 1911 and 1949, a Bill that deals only with taxation or expenditure must become law within one month of being sent to the Lords, whether or not they agree to it, unless the Commons directs otherwise. If no agreement is reached between the two Houses on a nonfinancial Commons Bill the Lords can delay the Bill for a period which, in practice, amounts to at least 13 months. Following this the Bill may be submitted to the Queen for Royal Assent, provided it has been passed a second time by the Commons. The Parliament Acts make one important exception: any Bill to lengthen the life of a Parliament requires the full assent of both Houses in the normal way.

The limits to the power of the Lords, contained in the Parliament Acts, are based on the belief that nowadays the main legislative function of the non-elected House is to act as a chamber of revision, complementing but not rivalling the elected House.

Delegated Legislation

In order to reduce unnecessary pressure on parliamentary time, primary legislation often gives ministers or other authorities the power to regulate administrative details by means of secondary or 'delegated' legislation. To minimise any risk that delegating powers to the executive might undermine the authority of Parliament, such powers are normally delegated only to authorities directly accountable to Parliament. Moreover, the Acts of Parliament concerned usually provide for some measure of direct parliamentary control over the delegated legislation, by giving Parliament the opportunity to affirm or annul it. Certain Acts also require that the organisations affected must be consulted before rules and orders can be made.

A joint committee of both Houses reports on the technical propriety of these 'statutory instruments'. In order to save time on the floor of the House, the Commons also uses standing committees to debate the merits of instruments; actual decisions are taken by the House as a whole.

Private and Hybrid Bills

Private Bills are promoted by people or organisations outside Parliament (often local authorities) to give them special legal powers. They go through a similar procedure to public Bills, but most of the work is done in committee, where procedures follow a semi-judicial pattern. Hybrid Bills are public Bills which may affect private rights. As with private Bills, the passage of hybrid Bills through Parliament is governed by special procedures which allow those affected to put their case.

Parliamentary Committees

Committees of the Whole House

Either House may pass a resolution setting itself up as a committee of the whole House to consider Bills in detail after their second reading. The general rule that an MP or Lord may speak only once on each issue does not apply in committee.

Standing Committees

House of Commons standing committees debate and consider amendments to public Bills at the committee stage and, in certain cases, discuss them at the second reading stage. They include two Scottish standing committees, and the Scottish, Welsh and Northern Ireland Grand Committees. The party balance of each committee reflects as far as possible that in the House as a whole. The Scottish Grand Committee comprises all 72 Scottish members (and may be convened anywhere in Scotland). It may consider the principles of Scottish Bills referred to it at second reading stage and other matters concerning Scotland (see p. 68). The Welsh Grand Committee, with all 38 Welsh members and up to five others, considers Bills referred to it at second reading stage, and matters concerning Wales only (see p. 66). The Northern Ireland Grand Committee debates matters relating specifically to Northern Ireland. The Lords' equivalent to a standing committee, a Public Bill Committee, is rarely used; instead the committee stage of a Bill is taken by the House as a whole.

Select Committees

Select committees are appointed to examine a subject and to report their conclusions and recommendations. To help Parliament with the control of the executive by examining aspects of public policy and administration, 15 departmental committees have been established by the House of Commons to examine the work of the main government departments and related bodies. The Foreign Affairs Committee, for example, 'shadows' the work of the Foreign &

Commonwealth Office. The composition of the committees reflects party strength in the House.

Other regular commons committees include those on Public Accounts, European Legislation, Members' Interests, and the Parliamentary Commissioner for Administration (the 'Parliamentary Ombudsman'—see p. 35). There are also a number of 'domestic' committees which cover the internal workings of Parliament.

In their examination of government policies and administration, committees may question ministers, senior civil servants, and interested bodies and individuals. Through hearings and published reports, they bring before Parliament and the public an extensive body of fact and informed opinion on many issues, and build up considerable expertise in their subjects of inquiry.

In the House of Lords, besides the Appeal and Appellate Committees, in which the bulk of the House's judicial work is transacted (see p. 17), there are two major select committees (with several sub-committees) on the European Communities and on Science and Technology.

Joint Committees

Joint committees, with a membership drawn from both Houses, are appointed in each session to deal with Consolidation Bills and delegated legislation. The two Houses may also agree to set up joint select committees on other subjects.

Party Committees

In addition to the official committees of the two Houses there are several unofficial party organisations or committees. The Conservative and Unionist Members' Committee (the 1922 Committee) consists of the backbench membership of the party in the House of Commons. When the Conservative Party is in office, ministers attend its meetings by invitation and not by right. When the party is in opposition, the whole membership of the party may attend meetings. The leader appoints a consultative committee, which acts as the party's 'shadow cabinet'.

The Parliamentary Labour Party comprises all members of the party in both Houses. When the Labour Party is in office a parliamentary committee acts as a channel of communication between the Government and its backbenchers in both Houses. Half of its members are elected and the remainder are government representatives. When the party is in opposition the Parliamentary Labour Party is organised under the direction of an elected parliamentary committee, which acts as the 'shadow cabinet'.

Other Forms of Parliamentary Control

House of Commons

In addition to the system of scrutiny by select committees, the House of Commons offers a number of opportunities for the examination of government policy by both the Opposition and the Government's own backbenchers. These include:

—Question time, when for an hour on Monday, Tuesday, Wednesday and Thursday, ministers answer MPs' questions. The Prime Minister's question time is on Tuesday and Thursday. Parliamentary questions are one means of seeking information about the Government's intentions. They are also a way of raising grievances brought to MPs' notice by constituents. MPs may also put questions to ministers for written answer; the questions and answers are published in Hansard, the official report. There are about 50,000 questions every year.

—Adjournment debates, when MPs use motions for the adjournment of the House to raise constituency cases or matters of public concern. There is a half-hour adjournment period at the end of the business of the day, while immediately before the adjournment for each recess (Parliament's Christmas, Easter, spring and summer breaks) a full day is spent discussing issues raised by private members.

There are also adjournment debates following the passage, three times a year, of Consolidated Fund[6] or Appropriation Bills.[7] These take place after the House has voted the necessary supplies (money) for the Government.

In addition, an MP wishing to discuss a 'specific and important matter that should have urgent consideration' may, at the end of question time, seek leave to move the adjournment of the House. If leave is given, a debate—known as an emergency debate—is held, usually on the following day.

—The 20 Opposition days each session, when the Opposition can choose subjects for debate.

—Debates on three days in each session on details of proposed government expenditure chosen by the Liaison Committee.

Procedural opportunities for criticism of the Government also arise during the debate on the Queen's speech at the beginning of each session, during debates on motions of censure for which the Government provides time, and during debates on the Government's legislative and other proposals.

House of Lords
Opportunities for criticism and examination of government policy are provided in the House of Lords at daily question time and during debates on general motions.

[6] At least two Consolidated Fund Acts are passed each session authorising the Treasury to make certain sums of money available for the public service.

[7] The annual Appropriation Act fixes the sums of public money provided for particular items of expenditure.

Control of Finances

The main responsibilities of Parliament, and more particularly of the House of Commons, in overseeing the revenue of the State and payments for the public service, are to authorise the raising of taxes and duties, and the various objects of expenditure and the sum to be spent on each. It also has to satisfy itself that the sums granted are spent only for the purposes which Parliament intended. No payment out of the central government's public funds can be made and no taxation or loans authorised, except by Act of Parliament. However, limited interim payments can be made from the Contingencies Fund.

The Finance Act is the most important of the annual statutes, and authorises the raising of revenue. The legislation is based on the Chancellor of the Exchequer's Budget statement. This is made in November or December each year and includes a review of the public finances of the previous year, and proposals for future expenditure. Scrutiny of public expenditure is carried out by House of Commons select committees (see p. 30).

European Union Affairs

To keep the two Houses informed of EU developments, and to enable them to scrutinise and debate Union policies and proposals, there is a select committee in each House, and two Commons standing committees debate specific European legislative proposals. Ministers also make regular statements about Union business.

The Commons' Ability to Force the Government to Resign

The final control is the ability of the House of Commons to force the Government to resign by passing a resolution of 'no confidence'. The Government must also resign if the House rejects a proposal which the Government considers so vital to its policy that it has declared it a 'matter of confidence' or if the House refuses to vote the money required for the public service.

Parliamentary Commissioner for Administration

The post of Parliamentary Commissioner for Administration (the 'Parliamentary Ombudsman') was established by the Parliamentary Commissioner Act 1967. The Commissioner investigates, independently, complaints of alleged maladministration when asked to do so by MPs on behalf of members of the public. Powers of investigation extend to administrative actions by staff in central government departments and certain executive non-departmental bodies. They do not include policy decisions (which can be questioned in Parliament) and matters affecting relations with other countries. The Commissioner has access to departmental papers and reports the findings to the MP who presented the complaint. The Commissioner is also required to report annually to Parliament. He or she publishes details of selected investigations at quarterly intervals and may submit other reports where necessary. A Commons select committee oversees the Commissioner's work.

Parliamentary Privilege

Each House of Parliament has certain rights and immunities to protect it from obstruction in carrying out its duties. The rights apply collectively to each House and to its staff, and individually to each member.

The Executive

Her Majesty's Government

Composition of the Government

Her Majesty's Government is the body of ministers responsible for the administration of national affairs. The Prime Minister is appointed by the Queen, and all other ministers are appointed by the Queen on the recommendation of the Prime Minister. Most ministers are members of the House of Commons, although the Government is also fully represented by ministers in the House of Lords. The Lord Chancellor is always a member of the Lords.

The composition of governments can vary both in the number of ministers and in the titles of some offices. New ministerial offices may be created, others may be abolished, and functions may be transferred from one minister to another.

Prime Minister

The Prime Minister is also, by tradition, First Lord of the Treasury and Minister for the Civil Service. The head of the Government became known as the Prime Minister during the 18th century (see p. 3). The Prime Minister's unique position of authority derives from majority support in the House of Commons and from the power to appoint and dismiss ministers. By modern convention, the Prime Minister always sits in the House of Commons.

The Prime Minister presides over the Cabinet, is responsible for the allocation of functions among ministers and informs the Queen at regular meetings of the general business of the Government.

The Prime Minister's other responsibilities include recommending a number of appointments to the Queen. These include:

—Church of England archbishops, bishops and other Church appointments;

—senior judges, such as the Lord Chief Justice;

—Privy Counsellors (see p. 98); and

—Lord-Lieutenants.

They also include certain civil appointments, such as Lord High Commissioner to the General Assembly of the Church of Scotland, Poet Laureate, Constable of the Tower, and some university posts; and appointments to various public boards and institutions, such as the BBC (British Broadcasting Corporation), as well as various royal and statutory commissions. Recommendations are likewise made for the award of many civil honours and distinctions.

The Prime Minister's Office at 10 Downing Street (the official residence in central London) has a staff of civil servants who assist the Prime Minister. The Prime Minister may also appoint special advisers to the Office from time to time to assist in the formation of policies.

Departmental Ministers

Ministers in charge of government departments are usually in the Cabinet; they are known as 'Secretary of State' or 'Minister', or may have a special title, as in the case of the Chancellor of the Exchequer.

Non-departmental Ministers

The holders of various traditional offices, namely the Lord President of the Council, the Chancellor of the Duchy of Lancaster, the Lord Privy Seal, the Paymaster General and, from time to time, Ministers without Portfolio, may have few or no departmental duties. They are thus available to perform any duties the Prime Minister may wish to give them.

Lord Chancellor and Law Officers

The Lord Chancellor holds a special position, as both a minister with departmental functions and the head of the judiciary (see p. 78). The four Law Officers of the Crown are: for England and Wales, the Attorney General and the Solicitor General; and for Scotland, the Lord Advocate and the Solicitor General for Scotland.

Ministers of State

Ministers of State usually work with ministers in charge of departments. They normally have specific responsibilities, and are sometimes given titles which reflect these functions. More than one may work in a department. A Minister of State may be given a seat in the Cabinet and be paid accordingly.

Junior Ministers

Junior ministers (generally Parliamentary Under-Secretaries of State) share in parliamentary and departmental duties. They may also be given responsibility, directly under the departmental minister, for specific aspects of the department's work. The Parliamentary Secretary to the Treasury and other Lords Commissioners of the Treasury are the formal titles of the Government Whips (see p. 23).

Ministerial Salaries

The salaries of ministers in the House of Commons range from £45,815 a year for junior ministers to £64,749 for Cabinet ministers (from January 1994). In the House of Lords salaries range from £38,894 for junior ministers to £52,260 for Cabinet ministers. The Prime Minister receives £78,292 and the Lord Chancellor £120,179.

Ministers in the Commons, including the Prime Minister, receive a reduced parliamentary salary of £23,854 a year (which is included in the above figures) in recognition of their constituency responsibilities and can claim the other allowances which are paid to all MPs (see p. 18).

The Leader of the Opposition in the Commons receives a salary of £61,349 (including the reduced parliamentary salary); two Opposition whips in the Commons and the Opposition Leader and Chief Whip in the Lords also receive salaries.

The Cabinet

The Cabinet is composed of about 20 ministers (the number can vary) chosen by the Prime Minister and may include departmental and non–departmental ministers.

The functions of the Cabinet are policy-making, the supreme control of government and the co-ordination of government departments. The exercise of these functions is vitally affected by the fact that the Cabinet is a group of party representatives, depending upon majority support in the House of Commons.

Cabinet Meetings

The Cabinet meets in private and its proceedings are confidential. Its members are bound by their oath as Privy Counsellors not to disclose information about its proceedings, although after 30 years Cabinet papers may be made available for inspection in the Public Record Office at Kew, Surrey.

Normally the Cabinet meets for a few hours once a week during parliamentary sittings, and rather less often when Parliament is not sitting. To keep its workload within manageable limits, a great deal of work is carried on through the committee system. This involves referring issues either to a standing Cabinet committee or to an ad hoc committee composed of the ministers directly concerned. The committee then considers the matter in detail and either disposes of it or reports upon it to the Cabinet with recommendations for action.

The membership of all ministerial Cabinet committees is published. Where appropriate, the Secretary of the Cabinet and other senior officials of the Cabinet Office attend meetings of the Cabinet and its committees.

Diaries published by several former ministers have given the public insight into Cabinet procedures in recent times.

The Cabinet Office

The Cabinet Office is headed by the Secretary of the Cabinet (who is also Head of the Home Civil Service), under the direction of the Prime Minister. It comprises the Cabinet Secretariat and the Office of Public Service and Science.

The Cabinet Secretariat serves ministers collectively in the conduct of Cabinet business, and in the co-ordination of policy at the highest level.

The Office of Public Service and Science is responsible for:

—raising the standard of public services across the public sector through the Citizen's Charter (see p. 46);

—improving the effectiveness and efficiency of central government, through, among other things, the establishment of executive agencies and the market testing programme (see p. 46); and

—advice—through its Office of Science and Technology—on science and technology policy, expenditure and the allocation of resources to the research councils.

It also promotes openness in government.

The Historical and Records Section of the Cabinet Office is responsible for Official Histories and managing Cabinet Office records.

Ministerial Responsibility

'Ministerial responsibility' refers both to the collective responsibility for government policy and actions, which ministers share, and to ministers' individual responsibility for their departments' work.

The doctrine of collective responsibility means that the Cabinet acts unanimously even when Cabinet ministers do not all agree on a subject. The policy of departmental ministers must be consistent with the policy of the Government as a whole. Once the Government's policy on a matter has been decided, each minister is expected to support it or resign. On rare occasions, ministers have been allowed free votes in Parliament on government policies involving important issues of principle.

The individual responsibility of ministers for the work of their departments means that they are answerable to Parliament for all their departments' activities. They bear the consequences of any failure in administration, any injustice to an individual or any aspect of policy which may be criticised in Parliament, whether personally responsible or not. Since most ministers are members of the House of Commons, they must answer questions and defend themselves against criticism in person. Departmental ministers in the House of Lords are represented in the Commons by someone qualified to speak on their behalf, usually a junior minister.

Departmental ministers normally decide all matters within their responsibility. However, on important political matters they usually consult their colleagues collectively, either through the Cabinet or through a Cabinet committee. A decision by a departmental minister binds the Government as a whole.

On assuming office ministers must resign directorships in private and public companies, and must ensure that there is no conflict between their public duties and private interests.

Government Departments

Government departments and their agencies are the main instruments for implementing government policy when Parliament has passed the necessary legislation, and for advising ministers. They often work alongside local authorities, statutory boards, and government-sponsored organisations operating under various degrees of government control.

A change of government does not necessarily affect the number or general functions of government departments, although major changes in policy may be accompanied by organisational changes.

The work of some departments (for instance, the Ministry of Defence) covers Britain as a whole. Other departments (such as the Department of Employment) cover England, Wales and Scotland, but not Northern Ireland. Others, such as the Department of the Environment, are mainly concerned with affairs in England. Some departments, such as the Department of Trade and Industry, maintain a regional organisation, and some which have direct contact with the public throughout the country (for example, the Department of Employment) also have local offices.

Departments are usually headed by ministers. Certain departments in which questions of policy do not normally arise are headed by permanent officials, and ministers with other duties are responsible for them to Parliament. For instance, ministers in the Treasury are responsible for HM Customs and Excise, the Inland Revenue, the National Investment and Loans Office and a number of other departments as well as executive agencies such as the Royal Mint. Departments generally receive their funds directly out of money provided by Parliament and are staffed by members of the Civil Service.

The functions of the main government departments are set out in Appendix 1 (see p. 87). The work of the Welsh, Scottish and Northern Ireland Offices is covered on pages 66–7, 68–71, and 72–6.

Non-departmental Public Bodies

A number of bodies with a role in the process of government are neither government departments nor part of a department (in April 1993 there were 1,389). There are three kinds of non-departmental public bodies: executive bodies, advisory bodies and tribunals. Tribunals are a specialised group of judicial bodies (see p. 80).

Executive Bodies

Executive bodies normally employ their own staff and have their own budget. They are public organisations whose duties include executive, administrative, regulatory or commercial functions. They normally operate within broad policy guidelines set by departmental ministers but are in varying degrees independent of government in carrying out their day-to-day responsibilities. Examples include the British Council, the Commonwealth Development Corporation and the Commission for Racial Equality.

Advisory Bodies

Many government departments are assisted by advisory councils or committees which undertake research and collect information, mainly to give ministers access to informed opinion before they come to a decision involving a legislative or executive act. In some cases a minister must consult a standing committee, but usually advisory bodies are appointed at the discretion of the minister. Examples include the Industrial Injuries Advisory Council and the Committee on Safety of Medicines.

The membership of the advisory councils and committees varies according to the nature of the work involved, but normally includes representatives of the relevant interests and professions.

In addition to the standing advisory bodies, there are committees set up by the Government to examine specific matters and make recommendations. For certain important inquiries Royal Commissions, whose members are chosen for their wide experience, may be appointed. Royal Commissions examine evidence from government departments, interested organisations and individuals, and submit recommendations. Some prepare regular reports. The Government may accept the recommendations in whole or in part, or may decide to take no further action or to delay action.

Examples of Royal Commissions include: the standing Royal Commission on Environmental Pollution, set up in 1970; the Royal Commission on the National Health Service, which was set up in 1975 and reported in 1979; and the Royal Commission on Criminal Justice, which was set up in 1991 and reported in 1993. Royal Commissions are often referred to by the names of the people who have chaired them.

Inquiries may also be undertaken by departmental committees.

Government Information Services

Each of the main government departments has its own information division, public relations branch or news department. These are normally staffed by professional information officers responsible for communicating their department's activities to the news media and the public (sometimes using publicity services provided by the Central Office of Information—see p. 97). They also advise their departments on the public's reaction.

The Lobby

As press adviser to the Prime Minister, the Prime Minister's Press Secretary and other staff in the Prime Minister's Press Office have direct contact with the parliamentary press through regular meetings with the Lobby correspondents. The Lobby correspondents are a group of political correspondents who have the special privilege of access to the Lobby of the House of Commons, where they can talk privately to government ministers and other members of the House. The Prime Minister's Press Office is the accepted channel through which information about parliamentary business is passed to the media.

Citizen's Charter

The Citizen's Charter was launched by the Prime Minister in 1991. The Charter's aim is to raise the standard of public services and make them more responsive to those who use them. It is closely linked to other reforms, including the Next Steps initiative, efficiency measures and the Government's contracting out and market testing programmes (see p. 49). The Citizen's Charter is a long-term programme which is intended to be at the heart of the Government's policy-making throughout the 1990s.

The Charter applies to all public services at both national and local levels and the privatised utilities. It sets out a number of key principles which users of public services are entitled to expect. All major public services are expected to publish separate charters, and so far 38 have been issued, including those for health, education and British Rail. In many cases separate charters have been published for services in Northern Ireland, Scotland and Wales.

Implementing the Charter

The mechanisms for implementing the Charter cover:

—more privatisation;

—wider competition;

—further contracting-out of service provision to private sector organisations;

—more performance-related pay for public sector staff;

—published performance targets;

—comprehensive publication of information on standards achieved;

—more effective complaints procedures;

—tougher and more independent inspectorates; and

—better redress for the citizen when things go wrong.

A Cabinet minister, the Chancellor of the Duchy of Lancaster, is responsible for the Charter programme. Implementation of the measures is co-ordinated by the Citizen's Charter Unit, within the Office of Public Service and Science.

A Charter Mark Scheme has been introduced to reward excellence in delivering services to the public: winners are judged by the Prime Minister's Citizen's Charter Advisory Panel. In 1993 awards were made to 93 of over 400 public services organisations and privatised utilities which had applied. Winners ranged from British Gas plc to schools, local authority services and executive agencies such as the Driver and Vehicle Licensing Agency.

Executive agencies are expected to comply fully with the principles of the Citizen's Charter, and the pay of agency chief executives is normally directly related to their agency's performance. Performance-related pay is being introduced throughout the service.

The Civil Service

The Civil Service is concerned with the conduct of the whole range of government activities as they affect the community. These range from policy formulation to carrying out the day-to-day duties of public administration.

Civil servants are servants of the Crown. For all practical purposes the Crown in this context means, and is represented by, the Government of the day. In most circumstances the executive powers of the Crown are exercised by, and on the advice of, Her Majesty's Ministers, who are in turn answerable to Parliament.

The Civil Service as such has no constitutional responsibility separate from the Government of the day, which it serves as a whole, that is to say Her Majesty's Ministers collectively. The duty of the individual civil servant is first and foremost to the Minister of the Crown who is in charge of the Department concerned. A change of minister, for whatever reason, does not involve a change of staff. Ministers sometimes appoint special advisers from outside the Civil Service. The advisers are normally paid from public funds, but their appointments come to an end when the Government's term of office finishes, or when the Minister concerned leaves the Government or moves to another appointment.

The number of civil servants fell from 732,000 in April 1979 to 554,200 in April 1993, reflecting the Government's policy of controlling the cost of the Civil Service and of improving its efficiency. About half of all civil servants are engaged in the provision of public services. These include paying sickness benefits and pensions, collecting taxes and contributions, running employment services, staffing prisons, and providing services to industry and agriculture. Around a quarter are employed in the Ministry of Defence. The rest are divided between: central administrative and policy duties; support services; and largely financially self-supporting services, for instance, those provided by the Department for National Savings and the Royal Mint. The total includes about 51,000 'industrial' civil servants, mainly manual workers in government industrial establishments. Four-fifths of civil servants work outside London.

Civil Service reforms are being implemented to ensure improved management performance. These reforms include performance-related pay schemes and other incentives.

Executive Agencies: Next Steps Initiative

The aim of the Next Steps Initiative, which was launched in 1988, is to deliver government services more efficiently and effectively within available resources for the benefit of taxpayers, customers and staff. This has involved setting up, as far as practicable, separate units or agencies to perform the executive functions of government. Agencies remain part of the Civil Service but, under the terms of individual framework documents, they enjoy greater delegation of financial, pay and personnel matters. Agencies are headed by chief executives who are accountable to ministers but who are personally responsible for the day-to-day operations of the agency and for meeting the financial and quality of service targets which it is set. By December 1993, 92 agencies had been set up, together with 31 Executive Units of Customs and Excise and 33 Executive Offices of the Inland Revenue. Almost 348,000 civil servants—over 60 per cent of the Civil Service—work in organisations run on Next Steps lines.

Efficiency Measures

In 1991 the Government announced further proposals to extend competition and choice in the provision of public services. Savings in public expenditure are being sought by market testing and competitive tendering of many services carried out by government departments. Services are contracted out to the private sector whenever the evaluation of tenders indicates that better value for money can be achieved.

Central Management and Structure

Responsibility for central co-ordination and management of the Civil Service is divided between the Treasury and the Cabinet

Office (Office of Public Service and Science—OPSS). In addition to its other functions, the Treasury is responsible for the structure of the Civil Service. It is also responsible for recruitment policy and for controlling staffing, pay, pensions and allowances. The OPSS is under the control of the Prime Minister, as Minister for the Civil Service; and is responsible for the organisation, non-financial aspects of personnel management and overall efficiency of the Service. The function of official Head of the Home Civil Service is combined with that of Secretary to the Cabinet.

At the senior levels, where management forms a major part of most jobs, there are common grades throughout the Civil Service. These unified grades 1 to 7 are known as the Open Structure and cover grades from Permanent Secretary level to Principal level. Within the unified grades each post is filled by the person best qualified, regardless of the occupational group to which he or she previously belonged.

Below this the structure of the non-industrial Civil Service is based on a system of occupational groups. These groups assist the recruitment and matching of skills to posts and offer career paths in which specialist skills can be developed. Departments and agencies are being encouraged to develop their own pay and grading arrangements. They are expected to produce value-for-money benefits which are greater than those available through centrally controlled negotiation.

The Diplomatic Service
The Diplomatic Service, a separate service of some 6,650 or so people, divided between Diplomatic Service and Home Civil Service grades, provides the majority of the staff for the Foreign & Commonwealth Office (see p. 94) and at British diplomatic missions and consular posts abroad.

The Service has its own grade structure, linked for salary purposes with that of the Home Civil Service. Terms and conditions of service are in many ways comparable, but take into account the special demands of the Service, particularly of postings overseas. Members of the Home Civil Service and the armed forces, and individuals from the private sector, may also serve in the Foreign & Commonwealth Office and at overseas posts on loan or attachment.

Recruitment

Recruitment is based on the principle of selection on merit by fair and open competition. Independent Civil Service Commissioners are responsible for approving the selection of people for appointment to the higher levels and to the fast stream entry of the Home Civil Service and the Diplomatic Service. Recruitment of middle-ranking and junior staff is the responsibility of departments and executive agencies; it is monitored by the Commissioners. Departments and agencies can choose whether to undertake this recruitment work themselves, to employ a private sector recruitment agency or to use the Recruitment and Assessment Services Agency to recruit on their behalf.

People from outside the Civil Service may be recruited directly to all levels, including the higher levels in the Open Structure, particularly to posts requiring skills and experience more readily found in the private sector.

Training

Individual government departments and agencies are responsible for the performance of their own staff. They provide training and development to meet their business needs, improve performance, and help staff respond effectively to changing demands. Most training and development takes place within departments and agencies. The Civil Service College also provides management and professional training, mainly for those who occupy, or hope to occupy, relatively senior positions.

Civil servants under the age of 18 may continue their general education by attending courses, usually for one day a week ('day release' schemes). All staff may be entitled to financial support to continue their education, mainly in their own time.

Promotion

Departments are responsible for promotion up to and including Grade 4. Promotion or appointment to Grades 1 and 2 and all transfers between departments at these levels are approved by the Prime Minister, who is advised by the Head of the Home Civil Service. Promotions and appointments to Grade 3 are approved by the Cabinet Office.

Political and Private Activities

Civil servants are required to perform loyally the duties assigned to them by the Government of the day, whatever its political persuasion. It is essential that ministers and the public should have confidence that the personal views of civil servants do not influence the performance of their official duties, given the role of the Civil Service in serving successive governments formed by different parties. The aim of the rules which govern political activities by civil servants is to allow them, subject to these fundamental principles, the greatest possible freedom to take part in public affairs consistent with their rights and duties as citizens. The rules are therefore concerned with activities liable to give public expression to political views rather than with privately held beliefs and opinions.

Security

Each department is responsible for its own internal security. As a general rule the privately-held political views of civil servants are not a matter of official concern. However, no one may be employed in connection with work which is vital to the security of the State who is, or has been, involved in, or associated with, activities threatening national security. Certain posts are not open to people who fall into this category, or to anyone whose reliability may be in doubt for any other reason.

The Security Commission may investigate breaches of security in the public service and advise on changes in security procedure, if requested to do so by the Prime Minister after consultation with the Leader of the Opposition.

Local Government

Although Britain's system of local government has its origins in structures developed in Saxon England (see p. 2), the first comprehensive system of local councils was established in the late 19th century. Over the years the range of services for which local authorities are responsible has grown and this has been one of the factors which has led to reforms in the pattern of local government.

Local Government Reform

A major reform of local government took place in 1974 in England and Wales and 1975 in Scotland. It was felt at the time that, while for some services it was more efficient for local authorities to cover large areas or serve many people, other services were best organised through smaller units in order to meet the needs of individual communities. In England and Wales, functions were therefore allocated to two main tiers of local authority: outside London these were counties and the smaller districts. In Scotland functions were allocated on the mainland to regions and districts; single-tier authorities were introduced for the three Islands areas. In Northern Ireland changes were made in 1973 which left local authorities with fewer functions than in the rest of Britain.

The Local Government Act 1985 abolished the Greater London Council and the six metropolitan county councils in England. In 1986 most of their functions were transferred to the London boroughs and metropolitan district councils respectively (see p. 56).

More recently the Local Government Act 1992 made provision for the establishment of a Local Government Commission to review the structure, boundaries and electoral arrangements of local government in England. The Commission is reviewing the structure of local government in all the English shire counties and is to complete its work by December 1994. The first changes are likely to be implemented in April 1995. It is expected that as a result of its reviews there will be a substantial increase in the number of unitary (single-tier) authorities in England, although there is no national plan.

Legislation to effect changes in Scotland and Wales is at present before Parliament. In Scotland the proposals would create 28 single-tier councils to replace the present system of regional and district councils. The three Islands councils would remain. In Wales it is proposed to set up 21 new unitary authorities to replace the existing two-tier structure (eight county councils and 37 district councils) in 1995.

Local Authorities' Powers

Local authorities' powers and duties are conferred on them by Parliament, or by measures taken under its authority. Administration is the responsibility of the local authority. In the case of certain services, however, ministers have powers to secure some national uniformity in standards in order to safeguard public health or to protect the rights of individual citizens. For some services the minister concerned has wide powers of supervision; in other cases the minister's powers are strictly limited.

Relations with Central Government

The main link between local authorities and central government in England is the Department of the Environment, although other departments such as the Department for Education and the Home Office are concerned with various local government functions. In the rest of Britain the local authorities deal with the Scottish and Welsh Offices and the Department of the Environment for Northern Ireland.

Principal Types of Local Authority

At present England and Wales (outside Greater London) are divided into 53 counties, sub-divided into 369 districts. All the districts and 47 of the counties—the 'non-metropolitan' counties—have locally elected councils with separate functions. County councils provide large-scale services, while district councils are responsible for the more local ones (see p. 60). Greater London—with a population of some 6.9 million—is divided into 32 boroughs, each of which has a council responsible for local government in its area; in addition, there is the Corporation of the City of London. In the six metropolitan counties there are 36 district councils; there are no county councils. A number of services, however, require a statutory authority over areas wider than the individual boroughs and districts. These are waste regulation and disposal (in certain areas); the police and fire services, including civil defence, and public transport (in all metropolitan counties); and the fire service, including civil defence (in London). All are run by joint authorities composed of elected councillors nominated by the borough or district councils.

In addition to the two-tier local authority system in England, there are over 8,000 parish councils or meetings. Historically, parishes date from medieval times, when they served as church boundaries, but they have operated as units of local government since 1894. They may provide and manage local facilities such as allotments and village halls and may act as agents for other district council functions. They also provide a forum for discussion of local issues. In Wales community councils have similar functions.

On the mainland of Scotland local government is at present on a two-tier basis; nine regions are divided into 53 districts, each of which has an elected council. There are three virtually all-purpose authorities for Orkney, Shetland and the Western Isles. Provision is also made for local community councils; although these have no statutory functions they can draw attention to matters of local concern.

The areas and electoral arrangements of local authorities in Wales and Scotland are kept under review by the Local Government Boundary Commissions for Wales and for Scotland. In 1992 the responsibilities of the Local Government Boundary Commission for England passed to the Local Government Commission.

In Northern Ireland 26 district councils are responsible for local environmental and certain other services. Statutory bodies, such as the Northern Ireland Housing Executive and area boards, are responsible to central government departments for administering other major services (see p. 61).

Election of Councils

Local authority councils consist of elected unpaid councillors. Councillors may, however, be entitled to a basic flat rate allowance and to certain expenses when attending meetings or taking on special responsibilities. Parish and community councillors cannot claim allowances for duties undertaken within their own council areas.

In England, Wales and Northern Ireland each council elects its presiding officer and deputy annually. Some districts have the ceremonial title of borough, or city, both granted by royal authority. In boroughs and cities the presiding officer is normally known as the Mayor. In the City of London and certain other large cities, he or she is known as the Lord Mayor. In Scotland the presiding officer of the district council of each of the four cities is called the Lord Provost. No specific title is laid down for those of other councils; some are known as conveners, while others continue to use the old title of 'provost'.

Councillors are elected for four years. All county councils in England and Wales, London borough councils, and about two-thirds of non-metropolitan district councils are elected in their entirety every four years. In the remaining districts (including all metropolitan districts) one-third of the councillors are elected in each of the three years between county council elections. In Scotland local elections are held every two years, alternately for districts and for regions and islands authorities. Each election covers the whole council so that councillors are elected for four years at a time.

Voters

Anyone may vote at a local government election in Britain provided he or she is:

—aged 18 years or over;

—a citizen of Britain or another Commonwealth country, or a citizen of the Irish Republic;

—not subject to any legal incapacity; and

—on the electoral register.

To qualify for registration a person must be resident in the council area on the qualifying date. In Northern Ireland there are slightly different requirements.

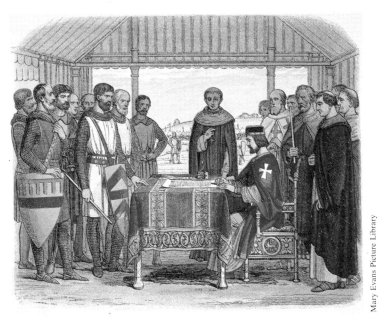

The signing of *Magna Carta* in 1215 (see p. 2).

A contemporary illustration depicting the alleged cruelty of the Cavaliers, the Royalist side, during the English Civil War (see p. 3).

The execution of King
Charles I in 1649,
following the defeat of
the Royalist side in the
Civil War (see p. 3).

King James II receiving the news
of the landing in England of
William of Orange during the
Revolution of 1688 (see p. 3).

The Palace of Westminster, showing the clock tower housing Big Ben.

The state opening of Parliament.

The Cabinet formed by the Rt Hon John Major, MP, the Prime Minister, in April 1992.

A civil servant from the Health and Safety Executive at work.

The Royal Courts of Justice in the Strand, in London.

A meeting of Liverpool City Council.

London Fire Brigade

Every part of Britain is covered by a local authority fire service which is
subject to some general oversight by central government.

Tynwald, the Isle of Man's parliament (see p. 105).

The States of Jersey in session (see p. 102).

Stormont, the headquarters of the Northern Ireland Office (see p. 75).

The European Parliament (see p. 84).

Candidates

Many candidates at local government elections stand as representative of one of the national political parties, although there are some independent candidates, and some represent local interests. Candidates must be British citizens, other Commonwealth citizens or citizens of the Irish Republic, and aged 21 or over. In addition, they must be registered as local electors, or live or work, in the area of the local authority to which they seek election.

No one may be elected to a council of which he or she is an employee, and there are some other disqualifications. All candidates for district council elections in Northern Ireland are required to make a declaration against terrorism.

Electoral Divisions

Counties in England and Wales are divided into electoral divisions, each returning one councillor. Districts in England, Wales and Northern Ireland are divided into 'wards', returning one councillor or more. In Scotland the electoral areas in the regions and islands areas are called electoral divisions, each returning a single member; the districts are divided into wards, similarly returning a single member. Parishes (in England) and communities (in Wales), may be divided into wards. Wards return at least one councillor.

Voting Procedure

The procedure for local government voting in Great Britain is similar to that for parliamentary elections. In Northern Ireland local government elections are held on the basis of proportional representation, and electoral wards are grouped into district electoral areas.

Council Functions and Services

At present county councils in England are responsible for strategic planning, transport planning, highways, traffic regulation, education (although schools may 'opt out' of local government control), consumer protection, refuse disposal, police, the fire service, libraries and the personal social services. District councils are responsible for local services such as environmental health, housing, decisions on most local planning applications, and refuse collection. Both tiers of local authority have powers to provide facilities such as museums, art galleries and parks; arrangements depend on local agreement.

In the metropolitan counties the district councils are responsible for all services apart from the police, the fire service and public transport and, in some areas, waste regulation and disposal (see p. 56). In Greater London the boroughs and the City Corporation have similar functions, but London's metropolitan police force is directly responsible to the Home Secretary. Responsibility for public transport lies with London Transport.

In Wales the division of functions between county and district councils is much the same as that between county and district councils in non-metropolitan areas of England.

Local authorities in England and Wales may arrange for any of their functions to be carried out on their behalf by another local authority, other than those relating to education, police, the personal social services and National Parks.

In Scotland the functions of regional and district authorities are, at present, divided up in a similar way to the counties and districts in England and Wales. Because of their isolation from the mainland, Orkney, Shetland and the Western Isles have single, virtually all-purpose authorities; they take part in wider-scale administration for their police and fire services, however, and rely on the mainland for assistance in the more specialised aspects of education and social work.

In Northern Ireland local environmental and certain other services, such as leisure and the arts, are administered by the district councils. Responsibility for planning, roads, water supply and sewerage services is exercised in each district through a divisional office of the Department of the Environment for Northern Ireland. Area boards, responsible to central departments, administer education, public libraries and the health and personal social services locally. The Northern Ireland Housing Executive, responsible to the Department of the Environment, administers housing.

Internal Organisation of Local Authorities

Local authorities have considerable freedom to make arrangements for carrying out their duties. The main policies are decided by the full council; other matters concerning the various services are the responsibility of committees composed of members of the council. A council may delegate to a committee or officer any function except those concerned with raising loans, levying local taxes or making financial demands on other local authorities liable to contribute. These powers are legally reserved to the council as a whole. The powers and duties of local authority committees are usually laid down in formal standing orders.

Parish and community councils in England and Wales are often able to do their work in full session, although they appoint committees from time to time as necessary.

Committees have to reflect the political composition of the council. In England and Wales people who are not members of the council may be appointed to decision-making committees and are able to speak and take part in debates; they cannot normally vote. The legislation also prevents senior officers and others in politically sensitive posts from being members of another local authority or undertaking public political activity. Some of these provisions have not been introduced in Northern Ireland.

Public Access

The public (including the press) are admitted to council, committee and sub-committee meetings, and have a right of access to a wide range of documents. Local authorities may exclude the public from meetings and withhold these papers only in limited circumstances.

Employees

Around 2.4 million people are employed by local authorities in Great Britain. These include administrative, professional and technical staff, teachers, firefighters, those engaged in law and order services, and manual workers. Nearly half of all local government workers are employed in the education service.

Although a few appointments must be made by all the authorities responsible for the functions concerned, councils are individually responsible within national policy requirements for determining the size and duties of their workforces. In Northern Ireland each council must by law appoint a clerk of the council as its chief officer.

Senior staff appointments are usually made on the recommendation of the committee or committees involved. Most junior appointments are made by heads of departments, who are also responsible for engaging manual workers. Pay and conditions of service are usually a matter for each council, although there are scales recommended by national negotiating machinery between authorities and trade unions.

Authorities differ in the degree to which they employ their own permanent staff to carry out certain functions or use private firms under contract. The Government's policy of promoting value for money is encouraging the use of private firms where savings can be made.

Local Authority Finance

Local government expenditure accounts for about 27 per cent of public spending. The Government has sought to influence local government spending as part of a general policy of controlling the growth of public expenditure. Since 1984 the Government has had powers to limit or 'cap' local authority budgets by setting a maximum amount for local authorities which have, in its view, set budgets which are excessive.

In 1992–93 expenditure by local authorities in Britain was about £69,800 million.

System of Finance

Local authorities in Great Britain (but not Northern Ireland) raise revenue from three main sources:

—central government grants,

—non-domestic rates, and

—the council tax.

In England, for example, these provided 56, 28 and 16 per cent respectively of the revenue of local authorities in 1993–94.

Non-domestic rates are a tax on the occupiers of non-domestic property. The rateable value of property is assessed by reference to annual rents and reviewed every five years. In England and Wales the non-domestic rate is set nationally by central government and collected by local authorities. It is paid into a national pool and redistributed to local authorities in proportion to their population. In Scotland non-domestic rates are levied by local authorities. In Northern Ireland rates are not payable on industrial premises or on commercial premises in enterprise zones.

Domestic property is subject to the council tax, which replaced the community charge in April 1993. Each dwelling is allocated to one of eight valuation bands, depending on its estimated open market value in April 1991. Tax levels are set by local authorities, but the relationship between the tax for each band is fixed. Discounts are available for dwellings with fewer than two resident adults. People on low incomes are entitled to rebates of up to 100 per cent on their tax bill.

In Northern Ireland rates—local domestic property taxes—are payable; they are collected by local authorities.

Expenditure

In 1992–93 education accounted for 44 per cent of local authorities' current expenditure in England, Scotland and Wales. Most of the remainder was spent on roads and transport; housing and other environmental services; law, order and protective services; and personal social services.

Local government capital expenditure is financed primarily by borrowing and by sales of land and buildings. These sources are supplemented mainly by capital grants from central government.

Control of Finance

Local councils normally have a finance committee to keep their financial policy under constant review. Their annual accounts must be audited by independent auditors appointed by the Audit Commission in England and Wales, or by the Commission for Local Authority Accounts in Scotland. In Northern Ireland this role is exercised by a local government audit section appointed by the Department of the Environment for Northern Ireland.

Local Government Complaints System

Citizens' allegations of injustice resulting from local government maladministration may be investigated by independent statutory Commissions for Local Administration (local government ombudsmen).

A report is issued on each complaint investigated and, if injustice caused by maladministration is found, the local ombudsman normally suggests a remedy. The council must consider the report and tell the commissioner what action it proposes to take.

In Northern Ireland a Commissioner for Complaints deals with similar complaints.

Administration of Welsh, Scottish and Northern Ireland Affairs

Wales

Following the Roman withdrawal from Britain in the fifth century and the invasions by the Angles, Saxons and Jutes from northern Europe, the Britons maintained an independent existence in Wales. The country remained a Celtic stronghold, but was subject to English influence. In the late 13th century Edward I of England launched a successful campaign to bring Wales under English rule. Wales was placed for the most part under the same laws as England and in 1301 Edward's eldest son—later Edward II—was created Prince of Wales, a title which is still normally given to the eldest son of the Sovereign. Following the accession to the English throne in 1485 of Henry VII of the Welsh House of Tudor, the Acts of Union of 1536 and 1542 united England and Wales administratively, politically and legally.

Today substantial administrative autonomy for Wales is centred on the Secretary of State for Wales, who is a member of the Cabinet and has wide-ranging responsibilities for the economy, education, welfare services and the provision of amenities. These are exercised through the Welsh Office (see p. 67). Wales is represented at Westminster by 38 Members of Parliament; special arrangements exist for the discussion of Welsh affairs (see p. 30).

In 1979 proposals for the establishment of an elected Welsh assembly in Cardiff to take over policy-making and executive powers from central government were rejected in a referendum held in Wales.

Local government in Wales is exercised through a system of elected authorities similar to that in England (see p. 56), and the legal system is identical with the English one (see pp. 77–81).

Welsh Office

Cathays Park, Cardiff CF1 3NQ. Tel: 0222 825111

Gwydyr House, Whitehall, London SW1A 2ER. Tel: 071 270 3000

Responsibilities

The Welsh Office is responsible for many aspects of Welsh affairs, including health, community care and personal social services; education, except for terms and conditions of service, student awards and the University of Wales; Welsh language and culture; agriculture and fisheries; forestry; local government; housing; water and sewerage; environmental protection; sport; land use, including town and country planning; countryside and nature conservation; new towns; and ancient monuments and historic buildings (through CADW: Welsh Historic Monuments—an executive agency).

The Department's responsibilities also include roads; tourism; enterprise and training; selective financial assistance to industry; the Urban Programme and urban investment grants in Wales; the operation of the European Regional Development Fund in Wales and other European Community matters; women's issues; non-departmental public bodies; civil emergencies; all financial aspects of these matters, including Welsh revenue support grant; and oversight responsibilities for economic affairs and regional planning in Wales.

Scotland

A united kingdom first emerged in Scotland in the ninth century. Throughout the Middle Ages there was intermittent warfare between Scotland and England. When the childless Elizabeth I of England died in 1603, James VI of Scotland was her nearest heir. He became, in addition, James I of England; and England, Wales and Scotland collectively became known as Great Britain. However, apart from the union of the crowns, England and Scotland remained separate political entities during the 17th century, except for a period of enforced unification under Oliver Cromwell in the 1650s (see p. 3). In 1707 both countries were joined together under the Act of Union, which created a single parliament for Great Britain. Scotland retained its own system of law and church settlement.

Today Scotland continues to have its own legal (see p. 79) and church systems; it also has wide administrative autonomy. Separate Acts of Parliament are passed for Scotland where appropriate, and there are special arrangements for considering Scottish business in Parliament (see p. 30). The distinctive conditions and needs of Scotland and its people are reflected in separate Scottish legislation on many domestic matters. Special provisions applying to Scotland alone are also inserted in Acts which otherwise apply to Britain generally.

The Secretary of State for Scotland, a Cabinet minister, has responsibility in Scotland for a wide range of economic and social functions (see p. 69). These are exercised through the Scottish Office, which has its headquarters in Edinburgh and an office in London.

Following an examination of Scotland's place in Britain which began in April 1992, the Government proposed a number of changes to the responsibilities of The Scottish Office. As a result responsibility for training policy in Scotland and the Scottish Arts Council was transferred to The Scottish Office in April 1994. In addition ownership of Highlands and Islands Airports would be transferred to The Scottish Office and the Government would also review the scope for transferring to The Scottish Office responsibilities for encouraging industrial innovation.

A proposal for an elected assembly in Scotland, on which a referendum was held in 1979, failed to gain the support of the required 40 per cent of the electorate to bring it into effect, even though a majority of those voting gave it their approval.

Local government generally operates on a two-tier basis broadly similar to that in England and Wales, but was established by separate legislation (see p. 60).

Scottish Office

St Andrew's House, Edinburgh EH1 3DG. Tel: 031 556 8400
Dover House, Whitehall, London SW1A 2AU. Tel: 071 270 3000

Responsibilities

The Scottish Office is responsible for a wide range of policy matters. These include agriculture and fisheries, education, law and order, environmental protection and conservation of the countryside, land-use planning, local government, housing, roads and certain aspects of transport services, social work and health.

The Secretary of State also has a major role in planning and development of the Scottish economy, and important functions relating to industrial development, including responsibility for financial assistance to industry.

The Secretary of State has overall responsibility for legal services in Scotland and is advised by the two Scottish Law Officers—

the Lord Advocate and the Solicitor General for Scotland (see p. 71).

In the list below, executive agencies are indicated by italics.

The Scottish Office's responsibilities are discharged principally through its five departments (which include five executive agencies) There are also four smaller departments: the *Registers of Scotland* and the *Scottish Record Office*, the General Register Office for Scotland and the Scottish Courts Administration, which is also responsible to the Lord Advocate for certain legal functions.

Relations with Other Government Departments

Other government departments with significant Scottish responsibilities have offices in Scotland and work closely with The Scottish Office.

Scottish Departments

An outline of the functions of the main Scottish departments is given below.

> **Scottish Office Agriculture and Fisheries Department**
>
> Promotion and regulation of the agricultural and fishing industries; safeguarding public, plant and animal health welfare; enforcement of fisheries laws and regulations through the *Scottish Fisheries Protection Agency*.
>
> **Scottish Office Education Department**
>
> Education (excluding universities); student awards; the arts, libraries, museums and galleries, Gaelic language; sport and recreation.

Scottish Office Environment Department
Environment, including environmental protection, nature conservation and the countryside; land-use planning; water supplies and sewerage; local government, including finance; housing; building control; protection and presentation to the public of historic buildings and ancient monuments through *Historic Scotland.*

Scottish Office Home and Health Department
Central administration of law and order (including police service, criminal justice, legal aid and the *Scottish Prison Service*); the National Health Service; fire, home defence and civil emergency services; social work services.

Scottish Office Industry Department
Industrial and regional economic development matters; co-ordination of Scottish Office European interests; employment; training; energy; tourism; urban regeneration; new towns; roads and certain transport functions, particularly in the Highlands and Islands.

Central Services
Services to the five Scottish departments. These include the Office of the Solicitor to the Secretary of State, The Scottish Office Information Directorate, Finance, Personnel Management and Office Management Divisions.

Lord Advocate's Department*
Fielden House, 10 Great College Street, London SW1P 3SL.
Tel: 071 276 3000

Provision of legal advice to the Government on issues affecting Scotland; responsibility for drafting government primary legislation relating to Scotland and adapting for Scotland other primary legislation. Provision of advice in matters of parliamentary procedure affecting Scotland.

Crown Office*
5–7 Regent Road, Edinburgh EH7 5BL. Tel: 031 557 3800
Control of all prosecutions in Scotland.

*Directly responsible to the Law Officers, not part of The Scottish Office.

Northern Ireland

In 1169 Henry II of England launched an invasion of Ireland; up until then the island had been independent of England. However, although a large part of the country fell under the control of Anglo-Norman magnates, England exercised little direct control of Ireland during the Middle Ages. The Tudor monarchs showed a much greater tendency to intervene in Ireland and in 1541 Henry VIII assumed the title of King of Ireland. During the reign of Elizabeth I a series of campaigns was waged against Irish insurgents. The main focus of resistance was the northern province of Ulster. With the collapse of this resistance in 1607, Ulster was settled by immigrants from Scotland and England.

Northern Ireland consists of six of the nine counties of the former province of Ulster. These remained part of Britain when, in 1922, the 26 counties of Southern Ireland became the Irish Free State, a self-governing state outside Britain. In 1949 the Irish Free State became the Irish Republic, a fully independent republic outside the Commonwealth.

Between 1921 and 1972 Northern Ireland had its own Parliament and Government, subordinate to the Parliament at Westminster. The domination of the Parliament by the Protestant majority population, descendants of the Scottish and English settlers, led to resentment among the Roman Catholic community, many of whom aspired to unity with the Irish Republic. These feelings were an important factor behind the civil rights movement which emerged in 1967. Some Protestants regarded the movement as a threat and street demonstrations were increasingly marked by sectarian disturbances. In 1969 the Northern Ireland Government called for the transfer of additional units of British army troops. British soldiers were soon called upon to help restore order and have remained in Northern Ireland to assist the civil power ever since.

The Northern Ireland Government had responsibility for local affairs but not for defence and the armed forces, foreign and trade policies, and taxation and customs. In 1972, with violence continuing, the British Government decided to assume direct responsibility for law and order. The Northern Ireland Government, unable to accept this, resigned, and the British Government assumed direct responsibility for its functions.

The British Government remains committed to the principle of a locally accountable administration acceptable to, and enjoying the support of, both sections of the community. In 1991 and 1992 the four main constitutional parties—the Ulster Unionists, Democratic Unionists, Social Democratic and Labour Party and the Alliance Party—had a series of political talks with the British and Irish Governments to see whether they could reach an agreement taking into account three sets of relationships relevant to the Northern Ireland problem: those within Northern Ireland, those within the island of Ireland, and those between the British and Irish governments. Although the talks ended in November 1992 without full agreement, the parties agreed that further discussions were necessary. These are continuing.

Relations with the Irish Republic

The 1985 Anglo-Irish Agreement created an Inter-governmental Conference where both governments discuss issues of common interest, such as cross-border co-operation in the security, social and economic fields. The Irish Government can put forward views and proposals on specified matters affecting Northern Ireland provided that these are not the responsibility of a devolved administration in Belfast. Each government retains sovereignty and full responsibility for decisions and administration within its own jurisdiction.

Joint Declaration
In December 1993 the Prime Minister, John Major, and his Irish counterpart, Albert Reynolds, signed a joint declaration setting out a framework of the political realities and constitutional principles which would inform the search for a political settlement. In it the British Government reaffirmed that it would continue to uphold the democratic wish of the majority of people in Northern Ireland on the question of union with the rest of Britain or a united sovereign Ireland. Britain's primary interest was to see peace, stability and reconciliation established by agreement among all the people living in Ireland. It would therefore work closely with the Irish Government to achieve an agreement embracing 'the totality of relationships' through dialogue and co-operation based on 'full respect for the rights and identities of both traditions in Ireland.'

The Irish Government stressed that it would be wrong to attempt to impose a united Ireland against the wishes of the majority in Northern Ireland. It acknowledged Unionist fears about some elements in the Irish Constitution and confirmed that, as part of a balanced constitutional accommodation, it would make changes which would fully reflect the principle of consent in Northern Ireland.

Both governments pledged that they would seek—together with the Northern Ireland constitutional parties through political dialogue—to create institutions and structures enabling the people of Ireland to work together in all areas of common interest and to build the trust needed to end past divisions.

Both governments emphasised that peace meant a permanent end to paramilitary violence. The Declaration said any political party which was committed to non-violence and had shown its willingness to abide by the democratic process was free to join in dialogue in due course between the Governments and the political parties on the way ahead.

Northern Ireland Office

Stormont, Belfast BT4 3ST. Tel: 0232 763255
Whitehall, London SW1A 2AZ. Tel: 071 210 3000

Responsibilities

The Secretary of State for Northern Ireland is the Cabinet minister responsible for Northern Ireland. Through the Northern Ireland Office the Secretary of State has direct responsibility for constitutional developments, law and order, security, and electoral matters. The work of the Northern Ireland departments, whose functions are listed below, is also subject to the direction and control of the Secretary of State. There is provision for Northern Ireland MPs to debate business relating to Northern Ireland in Parliament (see p. 30).

Local government is the responsibility of 26 district councils (see p. 57).

In the list below executive agencies are indicated in italics.

Department of Agriculture for Northern Ireland
Development of agricultural, forestry and fishing industries; rural development; veterinary, scientific and advisory services; administration of European Community support and other arrangements.

Department of Economic Development for Northern Ireland

Development of industry and commerce, as well as administration of government policy on tourism, energy, minerals, industrial relations, employment equality, consumer protection, health and safety at work, and company legislation. Administration of an employment service and training schemes through the *Training and Employment Agency* and assistance to industry, through the industrial Development Board for Northern Ireland.

Department of Education for Northern Ireland

Control of the five education and library boards and education as a whole from nursery to higher and continuing education, youth services; sport and recreation, cultural activities and the development of community relations within and between schools.

Department of the Environment for Northern Ireland

Environmental protection; housing; planning; roads; transport and traffic management; vehicle licensing and taxation (including the *Driver and Vehicle Testing Agency*); harbours, water and sewage; *Ordnance Survey of Northern Ireland*; maintenance of public records; certain controls over local government; and the *Rate Collection Agency*.

Department of Finance and Personnel

Control of public expenditure; liaison with HM Treasury and the Northern Ireland Office on financial matters, economic and social research and analysis; EC co-ordination; charities; *Valuation and Lands Agency*; policies for equal opportunities and personnel management, and management and control of the Northern Ireland Civil Service.

Department of Health and Social Services for Northern Ireland

Health and personal social services; social legislation; and the Office of the Registrar-General. Responsibility for the *Northern Ireland Child Support Agency*. The *Social Security Agency (Northern Ireland)* has responsibility for the administration of all social security benefits and the collection of National Insurance contributions.

The Judiciary and the Administration of the Law

Law

Although Britain is a unitary state, England and Wales, Scotland and Northern Ireland all have their own legal systems, with considerable differences in law, organisation and practice. However, a large amount of modern legislation applies throughout Britain. The law is divided into criminal law and civil law; the latter regulates the conduct of people in ordinary relations with one another. The distinction between the two branches of the law is reflected in the procedures used, the courts in which cases may be heard and the sanctions which may be applied.

The legal system of England and Wales comprises both an historic body of conventions known as common law and equity, and parliamentary and European Community legislation; the last of these applies throughout Britain. The origins of the common law lie in the work of the king's judges after the Norman Conquest of 1066. In seeking to bring together into a single body of legal principles the various local customs of the Anglo-Saxons, great reliance was placed on precedent: the reporting of cases, which assisted in establishing precedents, began in the 13th century. Common law, which continues to be deduced from custom and interpreted in court cases by judges, has never been precisely defined or codified. It forms the basis of the law except when superseded by legislation. Equity law is derived from the practice of petitioning the King's

Chancellor in cases not covered by common law; it consists of a body of rules and principles developed since medieval times and applied by the courts. The English legal system is therefore distinct from many of those of Western Europe, which have codes derived from Roman law.

European Community law is confined mainly to economic and social matters; in certain circumstances it takes precedence over domestic law. It is normally applied by the domestic courts, but the most authoritative rulings are given by the European Court of Justice (see p. 84).

The Judiciary

The judiciary is independent of the executive; its judgments are not subject to ministerial direction or control. The Prime Minister recommends the highest judicial appointments to the Crown.

The Lord Chancellor (see p. 17) is head of the judiciary (except in Scotland). His responsibilities include court procedure and the administration of all courts other than coroners' courts. He recommends all judicial appointments to the Crown—other than those recommended by the Prime Minister—and appoints magistrates. Judges are normally appointed from practising barristers, advocates (in Scotland) or solicitors.

The Courts

Criminal Courts

Summary or less serious offences, which make up the vast majority of criminal cases, are tried in England and Wales by unpaid lay magistrates—justices of the peace (JPs), although in areas with a heavy workload there are a number of full-time, stipendiary magistrates. More serious offences are tried by the Crown Court, presided over by a judge sitting with a jury. The Crown Court sits at about 90 centres and is presided over by High Court judges, full-time 'Circuit Judges' and part-time recorders.

Appeals from the magistrates' courts go before the Crown Court or the High Court. Appeals from the Crown Court are made to the Court of Appeal (Criminal Division). The House of Lords is the final appeal court in all cases.

Civil Courts

Magistrates' courts have limited civil jurisdiction. The 270 county courts have a wider jurisdiction; cases are normally tried by judges sitting alone. The 80 or so judges in the High Court cover civil cases and some criminal cases, and also deal with the appeals. The High Court sits at the Royal Courts of Justice in London or at 26 district registries.

Appeals from the High Court are heard in the Court of Appeal (Civil Division), and may go on to the House of Lords, the final court of appeal.

The Home Secretary

The Home Secretary has overall responsibility for the criminal justice system in England and Wales and for advising the Queen on the exercise of the royal prerogative of mercy to pardon a person convicted of a crime or to remit all or part of a penalty imposed by a court.

Scotland

The principles and procedures of the Scottish legal system (particularly in civil law) differ in many respects from those of England

and Wales. This stems, in part, from the adoption of elements of other European legal systems, based on Roman law, during the 16th century.

Criminal cases are tried in district courts, sheriff courts and the High Court of Justiciary. The main civil courts are the sheriff courts and the Court of Session.

The Secretary of State for Scotland recommends the appointment of all judges other than the most senior ones, appoints the staff of the High Court of Justiciary and the Court of Session, and is responsible for the composition, staffing and organisation of the sheriff courts. District courts are staffed and administered by the district and islands local authorities.

Northern Ireland

The legal system of Northern Ireland is in many respects similar to that of England and Wales. It has its own court system: the superior courts are the Court of Appeal, the High Court and the Crown Court, which together comprise the Supreme Court of Judicature. A number of arrangements differ from those in England and Wales. A major example is that those accused of terrorist-type offences are tried in non-jury courts to avoid any intimidation of jurors.

Tribunals

Tribunals are a specialised group of judicial bodies, akin to courts of law. They are normally set up under statutory powers which also govern their constitution, functions and procedure. Tribunals often consist of lay people, but they are generally chaired by someone who is legally qualified. They tend to be less expensive, and less formal, than courts of law. Independently of the executive, tribunals decide the rights and obligations of private citizens towards one another or towards a government department or other public authority. Important examples are industrial tribunals, rent tribunals and social security appeal tribunals. Tribunals usually consist of an uneven number of people so that a majority decision can be reached. Members are normally appointed by the government minister concerned with the subject, although the Lord Chancellor (or Lord President of the Court of Session in Scotland) makes most appointments when a lawyer chairman or member is required. In many cases there is a right of appeal to a higher tribunal and, usually, to the courts. Tribunals and advisory bodies do not normally employ staff or spend money themselves, but their expenses are paid by the government departments concerned. An independent Council on Tribunals exercises general supervision over many tribunals.

---

[8] For further details, see *Northern Ireland* (Aspects of Britain: HMSO, 1992).

Britain and the European Union

Background to Britain's Membership

After the second world war, the countries of Western Europe sought ways of working together to reconstruct their economies and to organise themselves in a way which would ensure that wars between them would not occur again. In 1952 Belgium, France, the Federal Republic of Germany, Italy, Luxembourg and the Netherlands established the supranational European Coal and Steel Community (ECSC). Although Britain decided not to participate, it established a form of association with the new body.

In 1957 the same six countries signed the Treaties of Rome, which established the European Economic Community (EEC) and the European Atomic Energy Community (EURATOM). Britain, along with six other countries, formed the European Free Trade Association (EFTA) in 1960. When it became clear that stronger links between EFTA and the European Community[9] were not being established, Britain began negotiations to join the Community in 1961. However, both these talks and a further application submitted in 1967 were blocked by French opposition.

Negotiations began again in 1970. The terms of entry were approved by Parliament in 1971. In 1972 Britain signed the Treaty of Accession, and on 1 January 1973 it became a member of the Community, at the same time as Denmark and the Irish Republic.

In 1974 the incoming Government renegotiated the terms of entry. It then recommended continued membership of the

---

[9] The European Community comprised the ECSC, the EEC and EURATOM.

Community. This recommendation was endorsed by large majorities in both Houses of Parliament. In a referendum held in June 1975, 67.2 per cent of voters supported continued membership.

Following agreement on the need to make improvements in European co-operation, a Single European Act was passed in 1986. Its provisions included the completion of the internal markets, an increased role for the European Parliament, and co-operation between member states on foreign policy.

Britain and its Community partners reached agreement on a Treaty on European Union at the European Council meeting in Maastricht in December 1991. The Treaty, which came into force on 1 November 1993, established the European Union, comprising the European Community and arrangements for intergovernmental co-operation on common foreign and security policies and on justice and home affairs.

Union Institutions

Council of the European Union

Major policy decisions are taken by the Council of the European Union. Member states are represented by the ministers appropriate to the subject under discussion.

The Presidency of the Council changes at six-monthly intervals; Britain assumed it for the fourth time from July to December 1992. In some cases decisions must be made unanimously; in others they are decided by a majority or a qualified majority, with votes weighted according to each country's size. Community policies are implemented by regulations, which are legally binding and directly applicable in all member countries, and directives, which are binding on member states but allow national authorities to decide on means of implementation.

Heads of Government of the member countries meet twice a year as the European Council. This takes important decisions and discusses EU policies and world affairs generally.

European Commission

The European Commission is composed of 17 commissioners (two from Britain) who are nominated by member governments and appointed by common agreement. It puts forward policy proposals, executes decisions taken by the Council of the European Union and ensures that Community rules are correctly observed. The Commission is pledged to act independently of national or sectional interests.

European Parliament

The European Parliament has 518 members; Britain, along with the other three larger member states—France, Germany and Italy—sends 81 elected members. (After elections to be held in June 1994 there will be 567 members, 87 from Britain.) It is consulted on a wide range of issues before the Council takes final decisions. The Commission can be removed from office as a whole by a two-thirds majority of all members of the Parliament. The Parliament adopts the Community's annual budget in agreement with the Council.

The European Parliament's legislative powers were increased by the Single European Act and the Maastricht Treaty.

Court of Justice

The Court of Justice consists of 13 judges. It interprets and adjudicates on the meaning of the treaties and on measures taken by the Council of the European Union and the Commission. It also hears complaints and appeals brought by or against Union institutions, member states or individuals and gives preliminary rulings on cases referred by courts in the member states. It represents the final authority on all aspects of Community law.

The Single European Act provided for a Court of First Instance to relieve the Court of Justice of a substantial part of its workload. The new court began working in 1989.

Court of Auditors

The Court of Auditors oversees the implementation of the Community's budget. It helps to counter waste and fraud. The Court consists of one member from each state.

Appendix 1: Government Departments and Agencies

An outline of the principal functions of the main government departments and executive agencies (see p. 49) is given below.

Each section is divided into Cabinet ministries and other departments. Executive agencies are normally listed under the relevant department, although in some cases they are included within the description of the departments' responsibilities.

The work of many of the departments and agencies listed below covers Britain as a whole. Where this is not the case, the following abbreviations are used:

—(GB) for functions covering England, Wales and Scotland;

—(E, W & NI) for those covering England, Wales and Northern Ireland;

—(E & W) for those covering England and Wales; and

—(E) for those concerned with England only.

The principal address and telephone number of each department are given. For details of the addresses of executive agencies see the Civil Service Year Book.

The Cabinet Office and the responsibilities of the Office of Public Service and Science—OPSS—are described on p. 40. The functions of the Welsh, Scottish and Northern Ireland Offices are outlined on pp. 66–76.

Cabinet Office (Office of Public Service and Science)
70 Whitehall, London SW1A 2AS Tel: 071 271 1234

Executive Agencies
Central Office of Information (see p. 97)
Chessington Computer Centre
Civil Service College
HMSO
Occupational Health Service
Recruitment and Assessment Services Agency

Economic Affairs

CABINET MINISTRIES
Ministry of Agriculture, Fisheries and Food
Whitehall Place, London SW1A 2HH Tel: 071 270 3000

Policies for agriculture, horticulture, fisheries and food; responsibilities for related environmental and rural issues (**E**); food policies.

Executive Agencies
ADAS (Agricultural Development and Advisory Service)
Central Science Laboratory
Central Veterinary Laboratory
Intervention Board
Pesticides Safety Directorate
Veterinary Medicines Directorate

Department of Employment
Caxton House, Tothill Street, London SW1H 9NF Tel: 071 273 3000

Employment policy; training policy, youth education and business start-up; vocational qualifications; health and safety at work; industrial relations; equal opportunities; co-ordinating government policy on issues of particular concern to women; statistics on labour and industrial matters (**GB**); the Careers Service (**E**); international representation on employment and training matters.

Executive Agency
Employment Service

Department of Trade and Industry
Ashdown House, 123 Victoria Street, London SW1E 6RB
Tel: 071 215 5000

Industrial and commercial affairs; promotion of new enterprise and competition; information about new business methods and opportunities; investor protection and consumer affairs. Specific responsibilities include innovation policy; regional industrial policy and inward investment promotion; small businesses; management best practice and business/education links; deregulation; international trade policy; commercial relations and export promotion; competition policy; company law; insolvency; radio regulation; patents and copyright protection **(GB)**; the development of new sources of energy and the Government's relations with the energy industries.

Executive Agencies
Accounts Services Agency
Companies House
Insolvency Service
Laboratory of the Government Chemist
NEL (National Engineering Laboratory)
National Physical Laboratory
National Weights and Measures Laboratory
Patent Office
Radiocommunications Agency

Department of Transport
2 Marsham Street, London SW1P 3EB Tel: 071 276 3000

Land, sea and air transport; domestic and international civil aviation; international transport agreements; shipping and the ports industry; marine pollution; regulation of drivers and vehicles (including road safety); regulation of the road haulage industry; transport and the environment. Motorways and trunk roads; oversight of local authority transport **(E)**. Sponsorship of London Transport **(E)**, British Rail **(GB)** and the Civil Aviation Authority.

Executive Agencies
Coastguard
Driver and Vehicle Licensing Agency
Driving Standards Agency
Highways Agency
Marine Safety Agency
Vehicle Certification Agency
Vehicle Inspectorate
Transport Research Laboratory

HM Treasury
Parliament Street, London SW1P 3AG Tel: 071 270 3000

The formulation and implementation of economic policy; the planning of spending and taxation; and the central framework of Civil Service management and pay. General oversight of the financial system.

OTHER DEPARTMENTS
HM Customs and Excise
New King's Beam House, 22 Upper Ground, London SE1 9PJ
Tel: 071 620 1313

Collecting and accounting for Customs and Excise revenues, including value added tax; agency functions, including controlling certain imports and exports and compiling trade statistics.

ECGD (Export Credits Guarantee Department)
2 Exchange Tower, Harbour Exchange Square, London E14 9GS
Tel: 071 512 7000

Provision of insurance for project exporters against the risk of not being paid for goods and services; access to bank finance for exports; insurance cover for new investment overseas.

Board of Inland Revenue
Somerset House, London WC2R 1LB Tel: 071 438 6622

Administration and collection of direct taxes; valuation of property (**GB**).

Executive Agency
Valuation Office

Paymaster: Office of HM Paymaster General
Sutherland House, Russell Way, Crawley, West Sussex RH10 1UH
Tel: 0293 560999

An executive agency providing banking services for government departments other than the Boards of Inland Revenue and Customs and Excise, and the payment of public service pensions.

Central Statistical Office
Great George Street, London SW1P 3AQ Tel: 071 270 3000

An executive agency preparing and interpreting key economic statistics needed for government policies; collecting and publishing business statistics; publishing annual and monthly statistical digests.

REGULATORY BODIES

The Office of Electricity Regulation (OFFER)
Hagley House, Hagley Road, Birmingham B16 8QG Tel: 021 456 2100

Regulating and monitoring the electricity supply industry; promoting competition in the generation and supply of electricity; ensuring that companies comply with the licences under which they operate; protecting customers' interests **(GB)**.

Office of Gas Supply (OFGAS)
Stockley House, 130 Wilton Road, London SW1V 1LQ
Tel: 071 828 0898

Regulating and monitoring British Gas to ensure value for money for customers, and granting authorisations to other suppliers of gas through pipes; enabling development of competition in the industrial market.

Office of the National Lottery (OFLOT)
2–4 Cockspur Street, London SW1Y 5DH Tel: 071 211 6000

Responsible for the grant, variation and enforcement of licences to run the National Lottery and promote lotteries as part of it.

Office for Standards in Education (OFSTED)
Elizabeth House, York Road, London SE1 7PH Tel: 071 925 6800

Monitoring standards in English schools; regulating the work of independent registered schools inspectors **(E)**.

Office of Telecommunications (OFTEL)
Export House, 50 Ludgate Hill, London EC4M 7JJ Tel: 071 634 8700

Monitoring telecommunications operators' licences; enforcing competition legislation; representing users' interests.

Office of Water Services (OFWAT)
Centre City Tower, 7 Hill Street, Birmingham B5 4UA
Tel: 021 625 1300

Monitoring the activities of companies appointed as water and sewerage undertakers **(E & W)**; regulation of prices and representing customers' interests.

Legal Affairs

CABINET MINISTRY
The Lord Chancellor's Department
Trevelyan House, 30 Great Peter Street, London SW1P 2BY
Tel: 071 210 8500

Administration of the Supreme Court (Court of Appeal, High Court and Crown Court), the county courts, and the magistrates' courts **(E & W)**, together with certain other courts and tribunals and the Council on Tribunals. Responsibility for the Northern Ireland Court Service; national archives (maintained by the Public Record Office—see below); the Public Trust Office and the Official Solicitor's Department.

All work relating to judicial and quasi-judicial appointments (see p. 78). Overall responsibility for civil and criminal legal aid, for the Law Commission and for the promotion of general reforms in the civil law. (The Home Office has important responsibilities for the criminal law.)

Lead responsibility for private international law. The Legal Services Ombudsman and the Advisory Committee on Legal Education and Conduct are independent of the Department but report to the Lord Chancellor. Except for the Northern Ireland Court Service, the Lord Chancellor's remit covers England and Wales only.

Executive Agencies
HM Land Registry
Public Record Office

OTHER DEPARTMENTS

Crown Prosecution Service
50 Ludgate Hill, London EC4M 7EX Tel: 071 273 8000

An independent organisation responsible for the prosecution of criminal cases resulting from police investigations, headed by the Director of Public Prosecutions and accountable to Parliament through the Attorney General, superintending minister for the service **(E, W & NI)**.

Legal Secretariat to the Law Officers
Attorney General's Chambers, 9 Buckingham Gate, London SW1E 6JP Tel: 071 828 7155

Supporting the Law Officers of the Crown (Attorney General and Solicitor General) in their functions as the Government's principal legal advisers **(E, W & NI)**.

The Attorney General, who is also Attorney General for Northern Ireland, is the Minister responsible for the Treasury Solicitor's Department (see below), and has a statutory duty to superintend the Crown Prosecution Service (see above), the Serious Fraud Office (see p. 93), and the Director of Public Prosecutions for Northern Ireland.

Parliamentary Counsel
36 Whitehall, London SW1A 2AY Tel: 071 210 6633

Drafting of government Bills (except those relating exclusively to Scotland); advising departments on parliamentary procedure **(E, W & NI)**.

HM Procurator General and Treasury Solicitor's Department
Queen Anne's Chambers, 28 Broadway, London SW1H 9JS
Tel: 071 210 3000

Provision of a legal service for a large number of government departments. Duties include instructing Parliamentary Counsel on Bills and drafting subordinate legislation; providing litigation and conveyancing services; and giving general advice on interpreting and applying the law **(E & W)**.

Executive Agency
The Government Property Lawyers

Lord Advocate's Department and Crown Office (see p. 71)

Serious Fraud Office
Elm House, 10–16 Elm Street, London WC1X 0BJ Tel: 071 239 7272

Investigating and prosecuting serious and complex fraud under the superintendence of the Attorney General **(E, W & NI)**.

External Affairs and Defence

CABINET MINISTRIES

Ministry of Defence
Main Building, Whitehall, London SW1A 2HB Tel: 071 218 9000

Defence policy and control and administration of the armed services.

Defence Agencies
Army Base Repair Organisation
Chemical and Biological Defence Establishment
Defence Accounts Agency
Defence Analytical Services Agency
Defence Animal Centre
Defence Operational Analysis Centre
Defence Postal and Courier Services Agency
Defence Research Agency

Defence Agencies (continued)
Duke of York's Royal Military School
Hydrographic Office
Meteorological Office
Military Survey
Naval Aircraft Repair Organisation
Queen Victoria School
RAF Support Command's Maintenance Group Defence Agency
Service Children's Schools (North West Europe)

Foreign & Commonwealth Office
King Charles Street, London SW1A 2AH Tel: 071 270 3000

Conduct of Britain's overseas relations, including advising on policy, negotiating with overseas governments and conducting business in international organisations, promoting British exports and trade generally; administering aid (see below). Presenting British ideas, policies and objectives to the people of overseas countries; administering the remaining dependent territories; and protecting British interests abroad and British nationals overseas, including the provision of consular facilities to British citizens overseas.

Executive Agency
Wilton Park Conference Centre

OTHER DEPARTMENTS

Overseas Development Administration
94 Victoria Street, London SW1E 5JL Tel: 071 917 7000

Responsibility for Britain's overseas aid to developing countries, for global environmental assistance, and also for the joint administration, with the Foreign & Commonwealth Office, of assistance to Eastern Europe and the countries of the former Soviet Union. Responsibility for overseas superannuation.

Executive Agency
Natural Resources Institute

Social Affairs, the Environment and Culture

CABINET MINISTRIES

Department for Education
Sanctuary Buildings, Great Smith Street, London SW1P 3BT
Tel: 071 925 5000

Formulates and promotes policies for education **(E)**; responsibility for the Government's relations with universities **(GB)**.

Executive Agency
Teachers' Pensions Agency

Department of the Environment
2 Marsham Street, London SW1P 3EB Tel: 071 276 3000

Policies for local government finance and structure, housing, construction, inner cities, environmental protection, water industry, energy efficiency, the countryside and rural areas, land use planning and the Government estate, including the Property Services Agency **(GB)**.

Executive Agencies
Building Research Establishment
Ordnance Survey (see p. 97)
Planning Inspectorate
Queen Elizabeth II Conference Centre
Security Facilities Executive
The Buying Agency

Department of Health
Richmond House, 79 Whitehall, London SW1A 2NS
Tel: 071 210 3000

National Health Service; personal social services provided by local authorities; and certain aspects of public health, including hygiene **(E)**.

Executive Agencies
Medical Devices Directorate
Medicines Control Agency
NHS Estates
NHS Pensions Agency

Home Office

50 Queen Anne's Gate, London SW1H 9AT Tel: 071 273 3000

Administration of justice; criminal law; treatment of offenders, including probation and the prison service; the police; crime prevention; fire service and emergency planning; licensing laws; regulation of firearms and dangerous drugs; electoral matters and local legislation (**E & W**). Gaming (**GB**). Passports, immigration and nationality; race relations; royal matters. Responsibilities relating to the Channel Islands and the Isle of Man.

Executive Agencies
Fire Service College
Forensic Science Service
HM Prison Service
United Kingdom Passport Agency

Department of National Heritage

2–4 Cockspur Street, London SW1Y 5DH Tel: 071 211 6000.

The arts (**GB**); public libraries; local museums and galleries; tourism; sport; heritage—including listing and scheduling buildings, and royal parks and palaces (**E**); broadcasting; press regulation; film industry; export licensing of antiques; the National Lottery.

Executive Agencies
Historic Royal Palaces Agency
Royal Parks Agency

Department of Social Security

Richmond House, 79 Whitehall, London SW1A 2NS
Tel: 071 210 3000

The social security system (**GB**).

Executive Agencies
Benefits Agency
Child Support Agency
Contributions Agency
Information Technology Services Agency
Resettlement Agency
War Pensions Agency

OTHER DEPARTMENTS AND AGENCIES

Central Office of Information
Hercules Road, London SE1 7DU Tel: 071 928 2345

An executive agency providing publicity material and other information services for government departments and publicly funded organisations.

HMSO (Her Majesty's Stationery Office)
St Crispins, Duke Street, Norwich NR3 1PD and Sovereign House, Botolph Street, Norwich NR3 1DN Tel: 0603 622211

An executive agency providing stationery, office machinery and furniture, printing and related services to Parliament, government departments and other public bodies. Publishing and selling government documents.

Ordnance Survey
Romsey Road, Maybush, Southampton SO9 4DH Tel: 0703 792000

An executive agency providing official surveying, mapping and associated scientific work covering Great Britain and some overseas countries.

Office of Population Censuses and Surveys
St Catherine's House, 10 Kingsway, London WC2B 6JP
Tel: 071 242 0262

A department responsible for administration of the marriage laws and local registration of births, marriages and deaths; provision of population estimates and projections and statistics on health and other demographic matters; Census of Population (**E & W**). Surveys for other government departments and public bodies (**GB**).

Appendix 2: The Privy Council

The Privy Council was formerly the chief source of executive power in the State; its origins can be traced back to the Curia Regis (or King's Court), which assisted the Norman monarchs in running the government. As the system of Cabinet government developed in the 18th century, however, much of the role of the Privy Council was assumed by the Cabinet (see p. 39). Some government departments originated as committees of the Privy Council.

Nowadays the main function of the Privy Council is to advise the Queen on the approval of Orders in Council, including those made under prerogative powers, such as Orders approving the grant of royal charters of incorporation, and those made under statutory powers. Responsibility for each Order, however, rests with the minister answerable for the policy concerned, regardless of whether he or she is present at the meeting where approval is given.

The Privy Council also advises the Sovereign on the issue of royal proclamations, such as summoning or dissolving Parliament. The Council's own statutory responsibilities, which are independent of the powers of the Sovereign in Council, include supervising the registration authorities of the medical and allied professions.

Membership of the Council (retained for life, except for very occasional removals) is accorded by the Sovereign, on the recommendation of the Prime Minister (or occasionally, Prime Ministers of Commonwealth countries) to people eminent in public life—mainly politicians and judges—in Britain and the independent monarchies of the Commonwealth. Cabinet Ministers must be Privy Counsellors and, if not already members, are admitted to membership before taking their oath of office at a meeting of the Council. There are about 400 Privy Counsellors. A full Council is summoned only on the accession of a new Sovereign or when the Sovereign announces his or her intention to marry.

Committees of the Privy Council

There are a number of Privy Council committees. These include prerogative committees, such as those dealing with legislation from the Channel Islands (see p. 101) and the Isle of Man (see p. 104), and with applications for charters of incorporation. Committees may also be provided for by statute, such as those for the universities of Oxford and Cambridge and the Scottish universities. Membership of such committees is confined to members of the current administration. The only exceptions are the members of the Judicial Committee and the members of any committee for which specific provision authorises a wider membership.

The Judicial Committee of the Privy Council is the final court of appeal for certain independent members of the Commonwealth, the British dependent territories, the Channel Islands and the Isle of Man. It also hears appeals from the disciplinary committees of the medical and allied professions and certain ecclesiastical appeals.

Administrative work is carried out in the Privy Council Office under the Lord President of the Council, a Cabinet minister.

Appendix 3: The Channel Islands and the Isle of Man

Relations with Britain

The distinction between the Channel Islands and the Isle of Man and other dependent territories has long been recognised by the British Government. In 1801, when government business connected with the colonies was transferred from the Secretary of State for the Home Department, business relating to the Channel Islands and the Isle of Man remained (and still rests) with the Home Secretary. Under the provisions of the British Nationality Act 1981 Channel Islanders and inhabitants of the Isle of Man enjoy full British Citizenship.

The British Government is responsible for the foreign relations and external defence of the Channel Islands and the Isle of Man, and the Crown has ultimate responsibility for their good government. The Crown acts through the Privy Council, on the recommendation of ministers operating in their capacity as Privy Counsellors. The island authorities are normally consulted when international agreements that might be binding on them as well as on Britain are under consideration by the British Government.

The Channel Islands and the Isle of Man are included by the Interpretation Act 1889 within 'the British Islands', and in the Merchant Shipping Acts trade with them is classed as 'Home Trade'. They use British currency together with locally issued currency in the same denominations.

Relations with the European Union

The position of the Channel Islands and the Isle of Man is governed by Articles 25–27 of the Act concerning the Conditions of Accession and by Protocol 3 to the Treaty of Accession. The Articles provide that the Community Treaties shall apply to the islands only to the extent described in the Protocol. The broad effect is that the islands are included in the European Union solely for customs purposes and for certain aspects of the Common Agricultural Policy.

The Channel Islands

The Channel Islands, situated off the north-west coast of France, are not part of Britain but dependent territories of the British Crown with their own legislatures (the States in Jersey, in Guernsey and in Alderney and the Chief Pleas in Sark), executives and judiciaries.

The Channel Islands consist of two Bailiwicks, Jersey and Guernsey. The latter includes the neighbouring islets of Herm and Jethou, together with Alderney and Sark. Each Bailiwick has a Lieutenant Governor, who is the personal representative of the Sovereign and the official channel of communication between Britain and the Island authorities. In both Jersey and Guernsey, the Bailiff, who is appointed by the Crown, presides over the Royal Court and the legislature and is the head of the Island administration.

The total population of the islands is about 145,500.

History

The islands became part of the Duchy of Normandy in the 10th and 11th centuries, becoming dependent territories of the English

Crown when their Duke, William, became King of England in 1066. When continental Normandy was overrun by the King of France in 1204, the islands remained in the hands of the King of England, who continued to govern them in his capacity as Duke of Normandy until he surrendered the title in 1259. Thereafter the sovereign continued to rule the islands as though he were Duke of Normandy, observing their laws, customs and liberties. These were later confirmed by the charters of successive sovereigns, which secured the islands their own judiciaries, freedom from the process of the English courts and certain other privileges. After the separation of the islands from Normandy, the local institutions were gradually moulded, largely on local initiative, to meet changing circumstances.

From 1204 onwards the islands were attacked and sometimes occupied by French forces on a number of occasions during hostilities between France and England. They were occupied by Germany during the second world war.

System of Government and Law

The people of the Channel Islands are, with the exceptions mentioned in this chapter, responsible for their own affairs. Almost all island domestic legislation is made by their own legislatures. Island laws require approval by the Queen in Council (see p. 98) and are examined by the Home Office, in consultation with other government departments. The Home Secretary, as the Privy Counsellor primarily responsible for matters relating to the islands, then advises the Privy Council on whether Her Majesty in Council should make an assenting Order. Thus while in domestic affairs the islands form virtually independent democracies, their legislatures do not consist of their assemblies alone but each consists of the Queen, the Privy Council and the assembly.

Legislation passed by the British Parliament does not apply to the islands unless it contains express provision or necessary implication to that effect, or unless it has been extended to the islands by means of an Order in Council, generally made under an enabling provision in the Act. Consultations are held with the island authorities before the legislation is applied to their territories. Merchant shipping, aerial navigation, wireless telegraphy and nationality are examples of subjects on which British legislation applies to the islands.

The members of the States of Jersey and the States of Guernsey are elected directly by universal suffrage. There are two representatives from Alderney in the States of Guernsey.

Until the outbreak of the second world war in 1939, Alderney was independent of Guernsey, although part of the Bailiwick. The island was evacuated in 1940. After the war, Guernsey took over responsibility for the airfield, education, health, immigration and the police services. The States of Alderney, which consists of an elected President and 12 elected members, still retains some legislative powers.

Although the States of Guernsey has power to legislate for Sark in some matters, Sark also has its own constitution, which is a unique mixture of feudal and popular government, with a hereditary 'Seigneur' at its head.

In addition to the States, Jersey and Guernsey have a system of local administration based on the parish (douzaine in Guernsey).

The basis of the laws of the Channel Islands is the common law of the Duchy of Normandy, as modified by local precedent and custom. In some respects, such as inheritance and bankruptcy, the law in the islands differs quite considerably from that in England. The Royal Courts in Jersey and Guernsey have full power to determine civil and criminal cases. In criminal cases appeal lies to the

Courts of Appeal, which are constituted as separate courts for each Bailiwick, although they have a common panel of judges appointed by the Crown. The Judicial Committee of the Privy Council is the final court of appeal for civil and criminal cases. By arrangement with the British Government, some custodial sentences passed by the island courts are served in Britain.

The Home Secretary advises the Sovereign on the exercise of the prerogative of mercy in judicial matters arising in the islands.

The Isle of Man

The Isle of Man, which is situated in the Irish Sea off the coast of Cumbria, is not part of Britain but a dependent territory of the British Crown, with its own legislature (the Court of Tynwald), executive and judiciary. The Lieutenant Governor is appointed by and serves as the representative of the Crown. The population is about 70,000.

History

The island, an ancient kingdom, was under the general suzerainty of the kings of Norway until 1266, when it was ceded to Alexander III, King of Scotland. For the following 150 years it was the subject of claims by successive sovereigns of England and Scotland.

The English claim eventually prevailed, although there was no formal annexation by the English Crown. In 1405 Henry IV granted the island to Sir John Stanley and his heirs (who later became Earls of Derby). The Derby Lordship lasted, with one short interval, until 1736, when the Lordship passed, by inheritance, to the Murray family, the Dukes of Atholl. The Atholl interests in the island were bought out by the Crown, by statute, between 1765 and 1825.

The Isle of Man Purchase Act 1765, known as the 'Revestment Act', placed the island under the direct administration of the Crown. In 1866 the Isle of Man Customs, Harbours and Public Purposes Act separated the Manx revenues from those of Britain and gave Tynwald a limited control over island expenditure, subject to the approval of the Treasury and to the veto of the Lieutenant Governor. These provisions, which made available the finance necessary for public works in the island, were linked with the institution of a popularly elected legislative body, the House of Keys (see p. 106), hitherto self-nominated but thereafter elected for a term of years. The island now has control of its own revenues, and responsibility for the provision of most services rests with Departments of Tynwald (see below).

System of Government and Law

The people of the Isle of Man are, in general, responsible for their own affairs, with the exceptions already mentioned, and almost all domestic legislation is made by Tynwald. The Lieutenant Governor has delegated power to grant Royal Assent to legislation dealing with domestic matters, and there is provision for those laws which transcend the frontiers of the island to be reserved for Royal Assent by the Queen in Council (see p. 98). Island laws are examined by the Home Office in consultation with other government departments in order to determine whether Royal Assent may properly be given. In the case of legislation which is to be reserved, the Home Secretary then advises the Privy Council whether Her Majesty in Council should make an assenting Order. Thus, while in domestic affairs the island forms a virtually independent democracy, its legislature does not consist of Tynwald alone but of the Queen, the Privy Council and Tynwald.

Legislation passed by the British Parliament does not apply to the island unless it contains express provision or necessary implication to that effect, or unless it has been extended to the island by means of an Order in Council, generally made under an enabling provision in the Act. Consultations are held with the Government of the Isle of Man before the legislation is applied to the island. Merchant shipping, aerial navigation, wireless telegraphy and nationality are examples of the subjects on which British legislation applies to the Isle of Man.

The Court of Tynwald, claimed to be 1,000 years old in 1979 and to be the oldest legislature in the world, consists of the Lieutenant Governor; the Legislative Council, which includes members indirectly elected by the House of Keys and certain ex officio members; and the House of Keys, an assembly of 24 members elected by universal adult suffrage. A Council of Ministers (formerly the Executive Council) appointed under the Council of Ministers Act 1990 from members of Tynwald acts in all matters of government. The Lieutenant Governor's earlier functions (for example, presiding over Tynwald and in government through the Governor in Council role) have now been removed.

The Manx judicial system has three tiers—the magistrates' courts (staffed by Justices of the Peace approved by the Lord Chancellor of England), the Manx High Court and the Manx Court of Appeal. The Judge of Appeal is appointed by the Crown. The Judicial Committee of the Privy Council is the final court of appeal for civil and criminal cases. The two Manx judges, who are also appointed by the Crown, are known as Deemsters (derived from their function of giving a 'doom' or judgment). By arrangement with the British Government, some custodial sentences passed by the island's courts are served in Britain. The Home Secretary advises the Sovereign on the exercise of the prerogative of mercy in judicial matters arising in the island. The Lieutenant Governor possesses delegated powers where the offender has been convicted and is serving his or her sentence on the island.

Further Reading

General

Aspects of Britain series

Britain's Legal Systems	HMSO 1993
Organisation of Political Parties	HMSO 1994
Pressure Groups	HMSO 1994

Other

The Administrative Process in Britain.
Brown, R. G. S. and Steel, D. R.
Second edition.   Methuen: Routledge 1979

British System of Government.
Birch, Anthony H. 9th edition.   Routledge 1990

Constitutional and Administrative Law.
Smith, S. A. De, Street, H. and Brazier, R.
7th edition.   Penguin 1994

Governing Britain: A Guidebook to
Political Institutions. Hanson, A. H.
and Walles, M.   Fontana Press 1990

Public Administration in Britain Today.
Greenwood, J. R. and Wilson, D. J.   Unwin Hyman 1989

Monarchy

The Monarchy (Aspects of Britain series).   HMSO   1991

The Royal Encyclopaedia:
The Authorised Book of the Royal Family.
Allison, Ronald and Riddell, Sarah (ed)   Macmillan   1991

The Oxford Illustrated History of the
British Monarchy. Cannon, John and
Griffiths, Ralph.   Oxford University Press   1988

Royal Heritage—The Reign of Queen Elizabeth II.
Plumb, J. H. and Wheldon, Huw.   Chancellor   1985

Report of the Royal Trustees.   HMSO   1993

Parliament

Factsheets on various aspects of the House of Commons and its work, including a list of MPs and ministers, are available free from the Public Information Office, House of Commons, London SW1A 0AA.

    Factsheets on various aspects of the House of Lords and its work are available free from the Journal and Information Office, House of Lords, London SW1A 0PW.

Parliament (Aspects of Britain).   HMSO   1994

The Commons under Scrutiny, Ryle, Michael
and Richards, Peter (editors).   Routledge   1988

Dod's Parliamentary Companion.
Dod's Parliamentary Companion Ltd.   Annual

The House of Lords.
Shell, Donald.   Harvester Wheatsheaf 1992

How Parliament Works. Silk, Paul
(with Walters, Rhodri).   Longman 1989

Member of Parliament: the Job of a Backbencher.
Radice, Lisanne, Vallance, Elizabeth
and Willis, Virginia.   Macmillan 1987

Parliament. Griffiths, J A G
and Ryle, Martin.   Sweet and Maxwell 1989

Parliament Today.
Adonis, Andrew.   Manchester University Press 1990

Parliamentary Elections
(Aspects of Britain series).   HMSO 1991

*Parliamentary Commissioner for
Administration: Annual Report.*   HMSO

Parliamentary Practice (A Treatise on
the Law, Privileges, Proceedings and
Usage of Parliament). May,
Sir Thomas Erskine. 21st edition,
edited by Clifford T. J. Boulton.   Butterworth 1989

The Times Guide to the House of Commons,
Wood, Alan and Wood, Roger. 1992.   Times Books 1992

Prime Minister, Cabinet, Government Departments and the Civil Service

The Civil Service (Aspects of Britain series). HMSO 1994

History and Functions of Government Departments (Aspects of Britain series). HMSO 1993

Cabinet. Hennessy, Peter Basil Blackwell 1986

British Government and Politics. 6th edition. Punnett, R. M. Dartmouth 1994

The Citizen's Charter. Raising the Standard. Cm. 1599. HMSO 1991

Citizen's Charter Annual Report. HMSO

Civil Servants and Ministers: Duties and Responsibilities. Government Response to the Seventh Report from the Treasury and Civil Service Committee, Session 1985–86. HMSO

Civil Service Commissioners' Annual Report HMSO

Civil Service Statistics. Annual. HMSO

The Civil Service Today. Drewry, Gavin and Butcher, Tony. Blackwell 1991

Civil Service Year Book. Annual. HMSO

The Government and Politics of Britain. Mackintosh, John P. Edited by P.G. Richards. 7th edition. Unwin Hyman: Routledge 1988

Improving Management in Government: The Next Steps.
(A report to the Prime Minister).   HMSO 1988

Making the Most of Next Steps: the Management
of Ministers' Departments and their Executive
Agencies. Report to the Prime Minister.   HMSO 1991

The Next Steps Agencies Review. Annual   HMSO

Open Government. Cm 2290   HMSO 1993

Public Bodies. Annual   HMSO

Quangos in Britain. Governments and
the Networks of Public Policy Making.
Barker, Anthony (editor).   Macmillan 1982

Reforming the Civil Service.
Fry, Geoffrey, K.   Edinburgh University Press 1993

Whitehall.   Secker and Warburg 1989

The Whitehall Companion. Dods   Annual

Local Government

The Conduct of Local Authority Business:
The Government Response to the Report of
the Widdicombe Committee of Inquiry.   HMSO 1988

A History of Local Government in the
Twentieth Century. Keith-Lucas,
Bryan, and Richards, Peter G.   Allen & Unwin 1978

The Local Government System.
Richards, Peter G.   Allen & Unwin 1983

The Internal Management of Local
Authorities in England. A Consultation Paper.
Department of the Environment 1991

Local Government Act. HMSO 1992

Local Government Financial Statistics
1990/91–1993/94. HMSO 1994

Local Government in Britain:
Everyone's Guide to How It All Works.
Byrne, Anthony. Fifth edition. Penguin 1990

Local Government in Wales:
A Charter for the Future. Cmnd 2155. HMSO 1993

Reviewing Local Government in the English Shires:
A Progress Report. HMSO 1993

A New Tax for Local Government. A Consultation
Paper. Department of the Environment 1991

Paying for Local Government. HMSO 1986

The Reform of Local Government Finance
in Britain. Bailey, S. J. and Paddison, R. (ed). Routledge 1988

Report of the Committee of inquiry into
the Conduct of Local Authority Business.
(Chairman: Mr David Widdicombe, QC.) HMSO 1986

Research Vol 1: The Political Organisation
of Local Authorities. HMSO 1986

Research Vol II:
The Local Government Councillor. HMSO 1986

Research Vol III:
The Local Government Elector. HMSO 1986

Research Vol IV:
Aspects of Local Democracy.   HMSO 1986

Scotland in the Union: A Partnership for Good
Cm 2225.   HMSO 1993

The Structure of Local Government in England. A
Consultation Paper.   Department of the Environment 1991

Index

Printed in the UK for HMSO.
Dd.0297871, 5/94, C30, 566734, 5673.